W9-BSR-756

8

Hollywood Knits

EX LIBRIS ·.· CARL B. MONTGOMERY

Hollywood Knits

BALLANTINE BOOKS • NEW YORK

EPIGRAPH

US COMMAND PERFORMANCE 1942

JUDY GARLAND TO BOB HOPE (MC)

*'Bob, why are men so crazy
about sweater girls?'*

BOB HOPE TO JUDY GARLAND

*'I don't know Judy, that's one mystery
I'd like to unravel.'*

Star profiles and line drawings © Bill Gibb 1987
Photographs from The Kobal Collection 1987
Knitting patterns and text © Pavilion Books Limited
1987

All rights reserved, including the right to reproduce this
book or portions thereof in any form, under
International and Pan-American Copyright
Conventions. Published in the United States by
Ballantine Books, a division of Random House, Inc.,
New York, and simultaneously in Canada by Random
House of Canada Limited, Toronto.

Library of Congress Catalog Card Number: 86-92103

ISBN 0-345-34661-0

Manufactured in Singapore
First American Edition: September 1987
Produced by Pavilion Books Limited, London
10 9 8 7 6 5 4 3 2 1

CONTENTS

Fly the flag with this longline cotton V-necked vest worked in stockinette stitch. The red, white and blue flag motif is worked from a simple chart and the ribbing is trimmed with garter stitch stripes in the same contrast colors.

· MEASUREMENTS ·

To fit bust 32(34,36,38,40)in/81(86, 91,97,102)cm
Actual measurements 35½(37½, 39½,41½,44)in/90(95,101,106,112)cm
Length to shoulders 26(26¼,26¾, 27¼,27½)in/66(67,68,69, 70)cm

· MATERIALS ·

7(7,8,8,9) × 50g balls Scheepjeswol Cotton Satin in main color A
1 ball of same each in contrast colors B and C
A pair each of size 3 (3¼ mm) and size 5 (4 mm) knitting needles

· GAUGE ·

22 sts. and 30 rows to 4 in (10 cm) over st.st. using size 5 (4 mm) needles.

· BACK ·

Using size 3 (3¼ mm) needles and A, cast on 99(105,111,117,123)sts.
Row 1: K1, * p1, k1, rep. from * to end.
Row 2: P1, * k1, p1, rep. from * to end.
Rep. these 2 rows once more.
Row 5: Using B, k to end.
Row 6: Using B, as row 2.
Row 7: Using B, as row 1.
Row 8: Using A, p to end.
Row 9: Using A, as row 1.
Row 10: Using C, p to end.
Rows 11 and 12: Using C, as rows 1 and 2.

VILMA BANKY

1902 ☞

Vilma Banky was born Vilma Lonchit in Nagyrodog, near Budapest. She had already made quite a few films in Europe before being discovered by Samuel Goldwyn on one of his talent-spotting tours and a five-year Hollywood contract was signed with him. She had all the physical requirements of a star: slender, golden-haired, graceful and ethereal, Vilma Banky was the essence of feminity.

One of Goldwyn's favorite stars, he promoted her as 'The Hungarian Rhapsody' and, no doubt partially as a publicity stunt, spared no expense on her wedding in 1927 to Rod la Rocque, which went down in the annals of Hollywood as one of its most legendary events.

In the 1920s Banky was teamed very successfully with the gentle, romantic Ronald Colman in her first Hollywood film *The Dark Angel* (1925). The partnership was dynamite and audiences demanded more and more of the Banky/Colman magic. They made five films together. Also in 1925, she starred opposite heart-throb Rudolph Valentino in *The Eagle* and in his last film the *Son of the Sheik*.

Banky enjoyed a splendid career, but like so many silent stars she failed to make a successful transition to the 'Talkies' because of her heavy Hungarian accent. Her film work came to a swift end and she took up golf, reaching professional standard!

She was a typical beauty of her time, promoting contemporary 1920s fashions with style and humor. Cloche hats emphasized her smouldering eyes and in her heyday she seduced many an audience.

Row 13: Using A, k to end.
Row 14: Using A, as row 2.
Rows 15 to 18: Using A, rep. rows 1 and 2 twice.
Change to size 5 (4 mm) needles.
Using A only and beg. k row, work in st.st. until back measures 18½ in (47 cm) from beg., ending with a p row.
Shape armhole
Bind off 4(5,6,7,8)sts. at beg. of next 2 rows.
Dec. 1 st. each end of next and every following alternate row until 75(77, 79,81,83)sts. remain.
Work even until armhole measures 6½(7,7½,8,8¼)in / 17(18,19,20,21)cm from beg. of shaping, ending with a p row.
Shape neck
Next row: K19(20,20,21,21), turn and leave remaining sts. on a spare needle. Work on first set of sts. as follows:
Next row: Bind off 2 sts., p to end.
Next row: Bind off 8(8,8,9,9)sts., k to end.
Next row: Bind off 2 sts., p to end: 7(8,8,8,8)sts.
Bind off.
Return to remaining sts.
With right side facing, slip first 37(37,39,39,41)sts. onto a holder, join A to next st. and k to end of row.
K 1 row, then complete to match first side of neck, reversing all shaping.

· FRONT ·

Work as given for back until front measures 12½ in (31.5 cm) from beg., ending with a p row.
Join on and cut off colors as needed.
Use separate small balls of yarn for each area of color and twist yarns together when changing color to avoid making a hole.
Reading odd numbered (k) rows from right to left and even numbered (p) rows from left to right, proceed to position patt. from chart as follows:
Row 1: K15(18,21,24,27)A, working

from chart k13A, 2B, 39A, 2B, 13A, then with A k15(18,21,24,27).

Row 2: P15(18,21,24,27)A, working from chart p14A, 2B, 37A, 2B, 14A, then with A, p15(18,21,24,27).

Continue working from chart in this way until row 46 has been completed.

Shape armhole

Bind off 4(5,6,7,8)sts. at beg. of next 2 rows.

Dec. 1 st. each end of next and every following alternate row until 85(89, 93,97,101)sts. remain, ending with a p row.

Shape neck

Next row: K2 tog, k40(42,44,46,48), turn and leave remaining sts. on a spare needle.

Work on first set of sts. as follows:

Work 1 row.

Dec. 1 st. at armhole edge as before and **at the same time** dec. 1 st. at neck edge on next and every following alternate row until 33 sts. remain.

Keeping armhole edge straight, continue dec. 1 st. at neck edge as before until 15(16,16,17,17)sts. remain.

Work even until front measures same as back to shoulder, ending at armhole edge.

Shape shoulder

Bind off 8(8,8,9,9)sts. at beg. of next row.

Work 1 row. Bind off.

Return to remaining sts.

With right side facing, slip first st. onto a safety-pin, join A to next st., then k to last 2 sts., k2 tog.

Work 1 row, then complete to match first side of neck, reversing all shaping.

· NECKBAND ·

Join right shoulder seam.

With right side facing and using size 3 (3¼ mm) needles and A, pick up and k50(52,54,56,58)sts. down left side of front neck, k the stitch from safety-pin

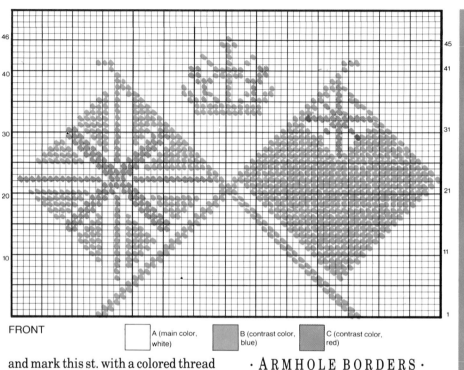

FRONT

A (main color, white)   B (contrast color, blue)   C (contrast color, red)

and mark this st. with a colored thread to denote center st., pick up and k50(52,54,56,58)sts. up right side of front neck and 5 sts. down right side of back neck, decreasing 1 st. at center k the sts. from back neck holder, then pick up and k5 sts. up left side of back neck: 147(151,157,161,167)sts.

Row 1: Using A, [k1, p1] to within 2 sts. of center st., skpo., p center st., k2 tog., [p1, k1] to end.

Row 2: Using A, rib to within 2 sts. of center st., skpo., k center st., k2 tog., rib to end.

Row 3: Using B, p to within 2 sts. of center st., p2 tog., p center st., p2 tog.tbl., p to end.

Row 4: Using B, as row 2.

Row 5: Using B, as row 1.

Row 6: Using A, k to within 2 sts. of center st., k2 tog.tbl., k center st., k2 tog., k to end.

Row 7: Using A, as row 1.

Row 8: Using C, as row 6.

Row 9: Using C, as row 1.

Row 10: Using C, as row 2.

Row 11: Using A, as row 3.

Using A, bind off loosely in rib.

· ARMHOLE BORDERS ·

Join left shoulder and neckband seam. With right side facing and using size 3 (3¼ mm) needles and A, pick up and k106(108, 112, 114, 118) sts. evenly round armhole.

Row 1: Using A, * K1, p1, rep. from * to end.

Row 2: Using B, k to end.

Row 3: Using B, as row 1.

Row 4: Using A, k to end.

Row 5: Using A, as row 1.

Row 6: Using C, k to end.

Row 7: Using C, as row 1.

Row 8: Using A, k to end.

Row 9: Using A, as row 1.

Using A, bind off loosely in rib.

· FINISHING ·

Join side and armhole border seams. Press lightly following instructions on ball band.

A	17¾	(18¾,	19¾,	20¾,	22)	in
	45	(47.5,	50.5,	53,	56)	cm
B	7½	(7¾,	8¼,	8¾,	9)	in
	19	(20,	21,	22,	23)	cm
C	16½					in
	42					cm
D	2					in
	5					cm
E	11	(11,	11½,	12,	12¼)	in
	28	(28,	29,	30,	31)	cm
F	1¼	(1½,	1½,	1½,	1½)	in
	3	(3.5,	3.5,	3.5,	3.5)	cm
G	6½	(7,	7¼,	7¾,	8)	in
	16.5	(17.5,	18.5,	19.5,	20.5)	cm

This long-sleeved, round-necked cardigan has puffed sleeves with turned back cuffs. It is worked in textured basketweave stitch with double ribbing. The neckband and borders are edged with a contrast yarn. Finish the cardigan with a scattering of embroidered flowers.

· MEASUREMENTS ·

To fit bust 30(32,34,36,38,40)in/76(81,86,91,97,102)cm
Actual measurements 35(36,38½,42, 44,46)in/88(92,98,106,112,116)cm
Length to shoulders 22¼ in (56 cm)
Sleeve seam (excluding cuff) 17½ in (44 cm)

· MATERIALS ·

6(6,6,7,7,7) × 50g balls in Lister Richmond D.K. in main color A
1 ball each of same in contrast colors B and C
A pair each of size 3 (3¼ mm) and size 5 (4 mm) knitting needles
Size F (4.00 mm) crochet hook
8 buttons

· GAUGE ·

19 sts. and 30 rows to 4 in (10 cm) over patt using size 5 (4 mm) needles.

· BACK ·

Using size 5 (4 mm) needles and A, cast on 84(88,94,100,106,110)sts.
Work in patt. as follows:
Row 1: Sl 1, k0(1,0,0,2,0), p3(4,0, 3,4,0), * k4, p4, rep. from * to last 8(2,5,8,3,5)sts., k4(2,5,4,3,5), p3(0,0, 3,0,0), k1(0,0,1,0,0).
Row 2: Sl 1, k3(0,0,3,0,0), p4(1,4, 4,2,4), * k4, p4, rep. from * to last 4(6,1,4,7,1)sts., k4(4,1,4,4,1), p0(1,0,

CLAUDETTE COLBERT

1905 ☞

Claudette Colbert, as her name suggests, was born in Paris. She was educated in New York where her parents moved when she was six, and became a stenographer, but she yearned to be an actress. She achieved this ambition on the New York stage, but was soon contracted to Paramount where she made innumerable movies. It was on loan from them to Columbia that she made one of the best films of her career, *It Happened One Night* (1934) with Clark Gable. Both won Oscars, much to her amazement, since she didn't relish her role as a runaway heiress plagued by a reporter, but the innovative treatment of this contemporary comedy established Colbert as a fine comedienne with a dry sense of humor and superb timing. With her versatile range, Cecil B. De Mille chose her to play the title role of *Cleopatra* (1934) – an epic on a grand scale which has Colbert scantily, but richly, clad and bejewelled slithering across super-shiny palace floors, scheming, pouting and using all her womanly wiles as befits Egypt's notorious Queen. In the 1940s she was one of Hollywood's highest paid stars.

Movie-goers loved her – she was confident and vulnerable at the same time, convincing with ease in tear jerkers or as a wicked *femme fatale*. She had a strange feline face, rounded cheeks, deep expressive eyes and an endearing smile. She was a superb clothes horse, so it was not surprising that even as a superstar she occasionally posed for fashion stills.

Claudette Colbert enjoyed a highly successful film career and was recently seen on the London stage, still able to captivate her audience.

0,2,0), k0(1,0,0,1,0).
Rows 3 to 6: Rep. rows 1 and 2 twice.
Row 7: Sl 1, p0(1,0,0,2,0), k3(4,0, 3,4,0), * p4, k4, rep. from * to last 8(2,5,8,3,5)sts., p4(1,4,4,2,4), k4(1,1, 4,1,1).
Row 8: Sl 1, p3(0,0,3,0,0), k4(1,4, 4,2,4), * p4, k4, rep. from * to last 4(6,1,4,7,1)sts., p3(4,0,3,4,0), k1(2,1, 1,3,1).
Rows 9 to 12: Rep. rows 7 and 8 twice.
These 12 rows form the patt.
Continuing in patt., work 12 rows.
Keeping patt. correct, dec. 1 st. each end of next and every following alternate row until 68(72,78,84,90,94)sts. remain, ending with a wrong-side row.
Work 8 rows even.
Keeping patt. correct, inc. 1 st. each end of next and every following alternate row until there are 84(88,94, 100,106,110)sts.
Work even until back measures 15 (14½,14½,14½,14,14)in /38(37,37,37, 36,36)cm from beg., ending with a wrong-side row.
Shape armholes.
Bind off 5 sts. at beg. of next 2 rows.
Keeping patt. correct, dec. 1 st. each end on next 5(7,9,12,13,15) rows: 64(64,66,66,70,70)sts.
Work even until armholes measure 7(7½,7½,7½,8,8)in/18(19,19,19, 20,20)cm from beg. of shaping, ending with a wrong-side row.
Bind off in patt.

· LEFT FRONT ·

Using size 5 (4 mm) needles and A, cast on 6(8,11,14,17,19)sts.
Work in patt. as follows:
Row 1: Sl 1, k0(1,0,0,2,0), p3(4,0,3, 4,0), [k4, p4] 0(0,1,1,1,2) times, k2.
Row 2: Sl 1, p1, [k4, p4] 0(0,1,1,1,2) times, k4(4,1,4,4,1), p0(1,0,0,2,0), k0(1, 0,0,1,0).
Row 3: Sl 1, k0(1,0,0,2,0), p3(4,0,3, 4,0), [k4, p4] 0(0,1,1,1,2) times, k2.

Row 4: Cast on 4 sts., k2, p4, [k4, p4] 0(0,1,1,1,2) times, k4(4,1,4,4,1), p0(1,0,0,2,0), k0(1,0,0,1,0): 10(12,15, 18,21,23)sts.

Row 5: Sl 1, k0(1,0,0,2,0), p3(4,0,3, 4,0), [k4, p4] 0(0,1,1,1,2) times, k4, p2.

Row 6: Cast on 4 sts., k1, p1, [k4, p4] 1(1,2,2,2,3) times, k4(4,1,4,4,1), p0(1,0,0,2,0), k0(1,0,0,1,0): 14(16,19, 22,25,27)sts.

Row 7: Sl 1, p0(1,0,0,2,0), k3(4,0,3, 4,0), [p4, k4] 1(1,2,2,2,3) times, p2.

Row 8: Cast on 4 sts., k1, p1, k4, [p4, k4] 1(1,2,2,2,3) times, p3(4,0,3,4,0), k1(2,1,1,3,1): 18(20,23,26,29,31)sts.

Row 9: Sl 1, p0(1,0,0,2,0), k3(4,0,3, 4,0), [p4, k4] 1(1,2,2,2,3) times, p4, k2.

Row 10: Cast on 4 sts., k2, [p4, k4] 2(2,3,3,3,4) times, p3(4,0,3,4,0), k1(2, 1,1,3,1): 22(24,27,30,33,35)sts.

Row 11: Sl 1, p0(1,0,0,2,0), k3(4,0,3, 4,0), [p4, k4] 2(2,3,3,3,4) times, p2.

Row 12: Cast on 2 sts., k4, [p4, k4] 2(2,3,3,3,4) times, p3(4,0,3,4,0), k1(2, 1,1,3,1): 24(26,29,32,35,37)sts.

Continuing in patt. as set, work 1 row even, then cast on 2 sts. at beg. of following row.

Work 1 row even, then inc. 1 st. at shaped edge on following 3 rows: 29(31,34,37,40,42)sts.

Inc. 1 st. at shaped edge on following 3 alternate rows, so ending at side edge: 32(34,37,40,43,45)sts.

Patt. 10 rows, dec. 1 st. at beg. of next and every following alternate row **at the same time** inc. 1 st. at end of next and every following alternate row: 32(34,37,40,43,45)sts.

Work 2 rows, dec. 1 st. at beg. of next row **at the same time** inc. 1 st. at end of next and at beg. of following row: 33(35,38,41,44,46)sts.

Work 4 rows decreasing 1 st. at beg. of next and following alternate row **at the same time** inc. 1 st. at end of next and following alternate row: 33(35, 38,41,44,46)sts.

Increasing 1 st. at end of first row, patt. 8 rows: 34(36,39,42,45,47)sts.

Increasing 1 st. at beg. of next and every following alternate row, patt. 16 rows: 42(44,47,50,53,55)sts.

Work even until front measures same as back to beg. of armhole shaping, ending with a wrong-side row.

Shape armholes

Next row: Bind off 5 sts., patt. to last st., k1.

Next row: Sl 1, patt. to last st., k1.

* Work 5(7,9,12,13,15) rows decreasing 1 st. at armhole edge on every row: 32(32,33,33,35,35)sts.

Work even until armhole measures 4(4½,4½,4½,5,5)in/10(11,11,11,12,12) cm from beg. of shaping, ending with a wrong-side row.

Shape neck

Dec. 1 st. at neck edge on next 14 rows: 18(18,19,19,21,21)sts.

Work even until armhole measures same as back to shoulder.

Bind off in patt. *

· RIGHT FRONT ·

Using size 5 (4 mm) needles and A, cast on 6(8,11,14,17,19)sts.

Work in patt. as follows:

Row 1: K2, [p4, k4] 0(0,1,1,1,2) times, p3(4,0,3,4,0), k1(2,1,1,3,1).

Row 2: Sl 1, p0(1,0,0,2,0), k3(4,0,3, 4,0), [p4, k4] 0(0,1,1,1,2) times, p2.

Row 3: Cast on 4 sts., k1, p1, k4, [p4, k4] 0(0,1,1,1,2) times, p3(4,0,3,4,0), k1(2,1,1,3,1): 10(12,15,18,21,23)sts.

Row 4: Sl 1, p0(1,0,0,2,0), k3(4,0,3, 4,0), [p4, k4] 0(0,1,1,1,2) times, p4, k2.

Row 5: Cast on 4 sts., k2, [p4, k4] 1(1,2,2,2,3) times, p3(4,0,3,4,0), k1(2, 1,1,3,1): 14(16,19,22,25,27)sts.

Row 6: Sl 1, p0(1,0,0,2,0), k3(4,0,3, 4,0), [p4, k4] 1(1,2,2,2,3) times, p2.

Row 7: Cast on 4 sts., k2, p4, [k4, p4]

1(1,2,2,2,3) times, k4(4,1,4,4,1), p0(1, 0,0,2,0), k0(1,0,0,1,0): 18(20,23,26, 29,31)sts.

Row 8: Sl 1, k0(1,0,0,2,0), p3(4,0,3, 4,0), [k4, p4] 1(1,2,2,2,3) times, k4, p2.

Row 9: Cast on 4 sts., k1, p1, [k4, p4] 2(2,3,3,3,4) times, k4(4,1,4,4,1), p0(1, 0,0,2,0), k0(1,0,0,1,0): 22(24,27,30, 33,35)sts.

Row 10: Sl 1, k0(1,0,0,2,0), p3(4,0,3, 4,0), [k4, p4] 2(2,3,3,3,4) times, k2.

Row 11: Cast on 2 sts., k1, p3, [k4, p4] 2(2,3,3,3,4) times, k4(4,1,4,4,1), p0(1, 0,0,2,0), k0(1,0,0,1,0): 24(26,29,32,35, 37)sts.

Row 12: Sl 1, k0(1,0,0,2,0), p3(4,0,3, 4,0), [k4, p4] 2(2,3,3,3,4) times, k4.

Continuing in patt. as set, cast on 2 sts. at beg. of next row.

Work 2 rows even, then inc. 1 st. at shaped edge on following 3 rows: 29(31,34,37,40,42)sts.

Inc. 1 st. at shaped edge on following 3 alternate rows, so ending at side edge: 32(34,37,40,43,45)sts.

Patt. 10 rows, inc. 1 st. at beg. of next and every following alternate row **at the same time** dec. 1 st. at end of next and every following alternate row: 32(34,37,40,43,45)sts.

Work 2 rows, inc 1 st at beg. of next row and at end of following row **at the same time** dec. 1 st. at end of next row: 33(35,38,41,44,46)sts.

Work 4 rows increasing 1 st. at beg. of next and following alternate row **at the same time** dec. 1 st. at end of next and following alternate row: 33(35,38, 41,44,46)sts.

Increasing 1 st. at beg. of first row, patt 8 rows: 34(36,39,42,45,47)sts.

Increasing 1 st. at beg. of first row, patt. 8 rows: 34(36,39,42,45,47)sts. rows: 42(44,47,50,53,55)sts.

Work even until front measures same as back to beg. of armhole shaping, ending with a right-side row.

Shape armholes

Next row: Bind off 5 sts., patt. to last st., k1.

Now complete to match left front from * to *

· SLEEVES ·

Using size 3 (3¼ mm) needles and A, cast on 44(44,44,44,48,48)sts.
Rib row 1: Sl 1, k2, * p2, k2, rep. from * to last st., k1.
Rib row 2: Sl 1, * p 2, k2, rep. from * to last 3 sts., p2, k1.
Rep. these 2 rows 15 times more, increasing 1 st. each end of last row: 46(46,46,46,50,50)sts.
Change to size 5 (4 mm) needles.
Work in patt. as follows:
Row 1: Sl 1, p0(0,0,0,2,2), * k4, p4, rep. from * to last 5(5,5,5,7,7)sts., k4, p0(0,0,0,2,2), k1.
Row 2: Sl 1, k0(0,0,0,2,2), p4, * k4, p4, rep. from * to last 1(1,1,1,3,3)sts., k1(1,1,1,3,3).
Rows 3 to 6: Rep. rows 1 and 2 twice.
Row 7: Sl 1, k0(0,0,0,2,2), * p4, k4, rep. from * to last 5(5,5,5,7,7)sts., p4, k1(1,1,1,3,3).
Row 8: Sl 1, p0(0,0,0,2,2), k4, * p4, k4, rep. from * to last 1(1,1,1,3,3)sts., p0(0,0,0,2,2), k1.
Rows 9 to 12: Rep. rows 7 and 8 twice.
These 12 rows form the patt.
Continue in patt., increasing and working into patt. 1 st. each end of next and every following 8th(12th, 12th,12th,12th,10th) row to 70(58,58, 56,62,64)sts., then every following 4th row until there are 78(80,80,84, 84,86)sts.
Work even until sleeve measures 19¾ in (50 cm) from cast-on edge, ending with a wrong-side row.
Shape top
Keeping patt. correct, dec. 1 st. each end of next and every following 4th row until 62(62,62,70,66,70)sts. remain.
Dec. 1 st. at beg. of next 6(6,6,14,10,14) rows: 56 sts.
Bind off in patt.

· FINISHING ·

Using B, embroider flowers in Lazy Daisy stitch, then using straight stitch and C, embroider stems as illustrated. Join shoulder seams. Sew in sleeves, pleating to fit at top.
Join side and sleeve seams.
Edging: With right side facing and using size F (4.00 mm) crochet hook, join on C at lower edge of right side seam and work 2 rows of sc up right front, round back neck, down left front and along lower edge, working 8 buttonloops evenly spaced up right front edge by working 2 ch and missing 2 sc for each loop.

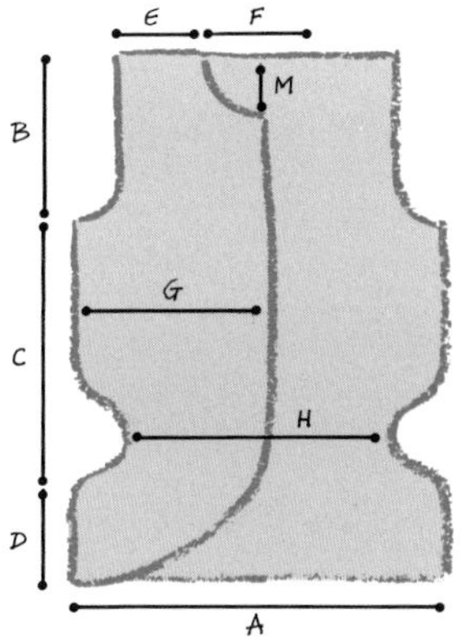

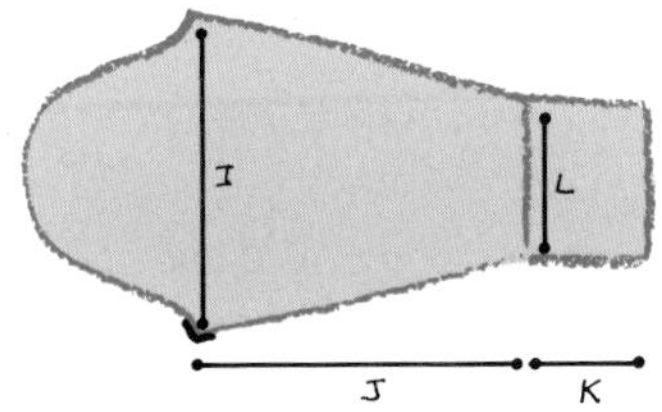

A	17½	(18,	19¼,	21,	22,	23)	in
	44	(46,	49,	53,	56,	58)	cm
B	7	(7½,	7½,	7½,	7¾,	7¾)	in
	18	(19,	19,	19,	20,	20)	cm
C	12	(11½,	11½,	11½,	11,	11)	in
	30	(29,	29,	29,	28,	28)	cm
D	3¼						in
	8						cm
E	3¾	(3¾,	4,	4,	4¼,	4¼)	in
	9.5	(9.5,	10,	10,	11,	11)	cm
F	6						in
	15						cm
G	8¾	(9,	9¾,	10¼,	11,	11½)	in
	22	(23,	25,	26,	28,	29)	cm
H	14¼	(15,	16,	17½,	18½,	19¼)	in
	36	(38,	41,	44,	47,	49)	cm
I	16	(16½,	16½,	17½,	17½,	17¾)	in
	41	(42,	42,	44,	44,	45)	cm
J	15¾						in
	40						cm
K	4						in
	10						cm
L	9½	(9½,	9½,	9½,	10¼,	10¼)	in
	24	(24,	24,	24,	26,	26)	cm
M	3¼						in
	8						cm

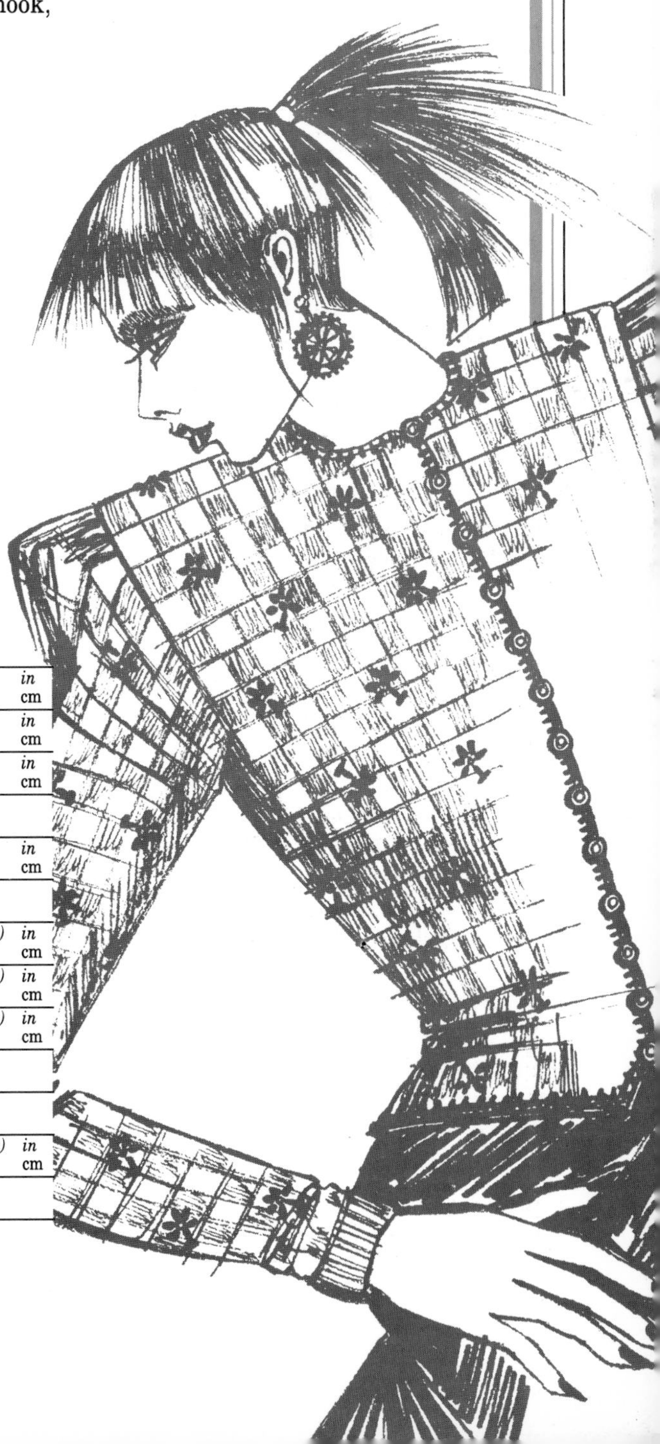

Here is a classic sportweight men's sweater with set-in sleeves and a round neck. Made in stockinette stitch, it has a simple Fair Isle design across the yoke and sleeves, worked from a chart. The yarn is machine washable for easy care.

· MATERIALS ·

9(10,10,11,12) × 50g balls Emu Superwash D.K. in main color A
2(2,2,3,3) balls in contrast color B
1(1,1,1,2) balls in contrast color C
A pair each of size 3 (3¼ mm), size 5 (4 mm) and size 6 (4½ mm) knitting needles

· MEASUREMENTS ·

To fit chest 36(38,40,42,44)in/91(97, 102,107,112)cm
Actual measurements 39½(41½,44, 45½,47½)in/101(106,112,116,121)cm
Length to shoulders 25¼(25¾,26, 26½,26¾)in/64(65,66,67,69)cm
Sleeve seam 19(19,19½,19½,20)in/48 (48,50,50,51)cm

· GAUGE ·

22 sts. and 30 rows to 4 in (10 cm) over st.st. using size 5 (4 mm) needles

· FRONT ·

* Using size 3 (3¼ mm) needles and A, cast on 101(107,113,117,123)sts.
Rib row 1: K1, * p1, k1, rep. from * to end.
Rib row 2: P1, * k1, p1, rep. from * to end.
Rep these 2 rows for 3 in (7.5 cm), ending with rib row 1.
Inc. row: Rib 6(8,8,10,8), * p.u.k., rib

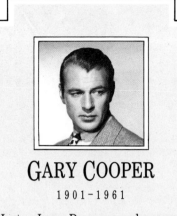

GARY COOPER
1901-1961

Just as James Dean emerged as a new kind of hero in the 1950s, so did Gary Cooper in the 1930s. His career spanned 35 years and he was undoubtedly one of the greatest film stars Hollywood had ever known. He was much admired by his peers who were unanimously of the opinion that the great secret of his acting was to appear not to be acting at all. He had a natural charm and extremely good looks, and exuded from the screen a powerful sexuality that won him millions of female fans. He was equally popular with men, who identified with his heroic qualities, virility and 'down to earth' attitudes.

Born in 1901 to British immigrants, Cooper originally intended to make a living from drawing, but unable to find a job, he became a film extra in Hollywood. He was snatched quickly from the crowd to play in *The Winning of Barbara Worth* (1926) which starred Vilma Banky. Within a few years he was a major star acting with many of Hollywood's most glamorous women – Lupe Velez in *Wolf Song* (1929), Marlene Dietrich in *Morocco* (1930), Joan Crawford in *Today We Live* (1933) and Grace Kelly in the classic western *High Noon* (1952).

His 'eternal classic' looks and relaxed poses are much emulated today by photographers for the glossy fashion magazines who demand Gary Cooper look-alikes. But underneath his cool nonchalant exterior lay a workman who planned his roles with great care and precision. Forty years on, he remains a true megastar of the film industry.

10(10,11,11,12), rep. from * to last 5(9,6,8,7)sts., p.u.k., rib 5(9,6,8,7): 111(117,123,127,133)sts.
Change to size 5 (4 mm) needles.
Proceed in st.st. until front measures 16(16, 16½,16½,17) in / 41 (41, 42, 42, 43) cm from beg., ending with a p row.

Shape armholes
Bind off 3(3,4,4,4)sts. at beg. of next 2 rows.
Dec. 1 st. each end of next and following alternate row: 101(107,111,115, 121)sts.
P 1 row.
Change to size 6 (4½ mm) needles.
Join on and cut off colors as required and carry yarn not in use loosely across wrong side of knitting.
Reading odd numbered (k) rows from right to left and even numbered (p) rows from left to right, work in patt. from chart 1, decreasing as indicated, until row 34 has been completed: 91(93,95,97,103) sts.
Change to size 5 (4 mm) needles.
Continuing in A only, work 2 rows st.st. *

Shape neck
Next row: K37(37,38,38,41), turn and leave the remaining sts. on a spare needle.
Dec. 1 st. at neck edge on next and every following alternate row until 24(24,25,25,27)sts. remain.
Work straight until the armhole measures 9(9½,9½,9¾,10)in /23(24,24,25, 26)cm from beg. of shaping, ending at the armhole edge.

Shape shoulder
Bind off 8(8,8,8,9)sts. at beg. of next and following alternate row.
Work 1 row. Bind off.
Return to remaining sts.
With right side facing, slip first 17(19,19,21,21)sts. onto a holder, join on A and k to end: 37(37,38,38,41)sts.
Now complete to match first side of neck.

GARY COOPER
1901-1961

· BACK ·

Work as given for front from * to *.
Continue even in st.st. until back measures the same length as front to beg. of shoulder shaping, ending with a p row.

Shape shoulders

Bind off 8(8,8,8,9)sts. at beg. of next 4 rows, and 8(8,9,9,9)sts. at beg. of following 2 rows.

Cut off yarn and leave remaining 43(45,45,47,49)sts. on a holder.

· SLEEVES ·

Using size 3 (3¼ mm) needles and A, cast on 45(47,49,51,53)sts.
Work the 2 rib rows for 3 in (7.5 cm), ending with rib row 1.

Inc. row: Rib 3(4,2,3,4), * p.u.k., rib 3, rep. from * to last 3(4,2,3,4) sts., p.u.k., rib to end: 59(61,65,67,69)sts.

Change to size 5 (4 mm) needles.
Proceed in st.st. increasing 1 st. each end of 9th and every following 6th row until there are 95(97,101,103,105)sts.
Work even until sleeve measures 19(19,19½,19½,20¼)in / 48(48,50,50, 51)cm from cast-on edge, ending with a p row.

Shape top

Bind off 3(3,4,4,4)sts. at beg. of next 2 rows.
Dec. 1 st each end of next and following alternate row: 85(87,89,91,93)sts.
P 1 row.
Change to size 6 (4½ mm) needles.
Work in patt. from chart, decreasing as indicated, until row 34 has been completed: 49(53,55,57,59) sts.
Change to size 5 (4 mm) needles.
Working in A only and continuing in st.st., bind off 2 sts. at beg. of next 2 rows and 5 sts. at beg. of following 4 rows.   Bind off.

· NECKBAND ·

Join right shoulder seam.
With RS facing, join A to neck at left shoulder and using size 3 (3¼ mm) needles, pick up and k22(24,25,28,30) sts. down left side of front neck, k the front neck sts. from holder, pick up and k22(24,25,28,30)sts. up right side of front neck, then increasing 1 st. at center k the back neck sts. from holder: 105(113,115,125,131)sts.
Beg. rib row 2, work 6 rows rib.
Bind off loosely in rib.

· FINISHING ·

Join left shoulder and neckband seam.
Set in the sleeves, then join side and sleeve seams. Press lightly.

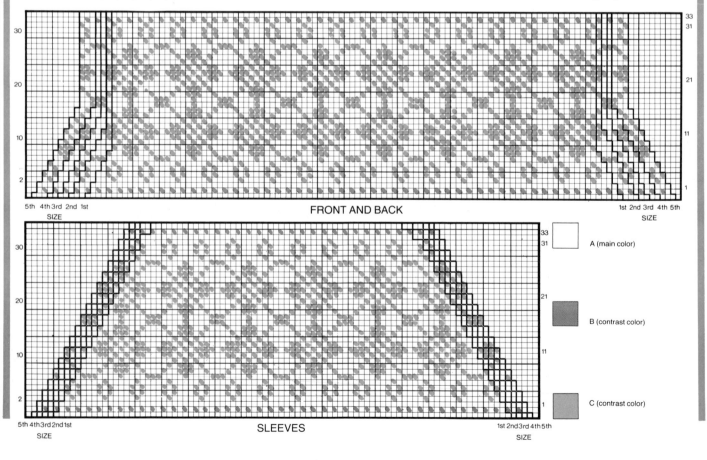

FRONT AND BACK

SLEEVES

A (main color)

B (contrast color)

C (contrast color)

A	20	(21,	22,	23,	24)	in
	51	(53.5,	56,	58.5,	61)	cm
B	9	(9½,	9½,	9¾,	10)	in
	23	(24,	24,	25,	26)	cm
C	13¼	(13¼,	13½,	13¾,	13¾)	in
	33.5	(33.5,	34.5,	35.5,	35.5)	cm
D	3					in
	7.5					cm
E	7½	(7¾,	7¾,	8¼,	8¾)	in
	19	(20,	20,	21,	22)	cm
F	3¼	(3½,	3½,	4,	4)	in
	8	(9,	9,	10,	10)	cm
G	17	(17½,	18,	18½,	19)	in
	43	(44,	46,	47,	48)	cm
H	6¾	(7,	7,	7½,	7¾)	in
	17	(18,	18,	19,	20)	cm
I	16	(16,	16½,	16½,	17¼)	in
	40.5	(40.5,	42.5,	42.5,	43.5)	cm
J	3					in
	7.5					cm
K	9	(9½,	9½,	9¾,	9¾)	in
	23	(24,	24,	25,	25)	cm

This smart but feminine pullover has short puffed sleeves and a simple round neck. The ribbing and cuffs are worked in double rib while the main fabric is in an attractive but simple variation of garter stitch with every row knitted – making for quick progress.

· MEASUREMENTS ·

To fit bust 30(32,34,36,38,40)in/76 (81,86,91,97,102)cm
Actual measurements 34(36,38,40, 42½,44½)in/86(91,96,100,107,112)cm
Length to shoulders 21 in (53 cm)
Sleeve seam 6 in (15 cm)

· MATERIALS ·

7 × 50g balls Lister Richmond D.K.
A pair each of size 3 (3¼ mm) and size 5 (4 mm) knitting needles

· GAUGE ·

17 sts. measure 4 in (10 cm) over pattern using size 5 (4 mm) needles.

· BACK ·

* Using size 3 (3¼ mm) needles cast on 84(88,96,100,108,112)sts.
Rib row 1: Sl 1, k2, * p2, k2, rep. from * to last st., k1.
Rib row 2: Sl 1, * p2, k2, rep. from * to last 3 sts., p2, k1.
Rep these 2 rows 10 times more, then rib row 1 again.
Dec. row: Sl 1, p0(2,4,6,4,6), * p2 tog., p6(6,4,4,4,4), rep. from * 9(9,13,13, 15,15) times more, p2 tog., p0(2,4,6, 4,6), k1: 73(77,81,85,91,95)sts.
Change to size 5 (4 mm) needles.
K 2 rows.
Proceed in patt. as follows:

JOAN CRAWFORD

1906–1977

Joan Crawford once said: 'I wouldn't copy anybody. If I can't be me I don't want to be anybody. I was born that way.' Certainly, this most durable of stars was not a copier or a follower of anybody or anything.

Born Lucille le Sueur on the wrong side of the tracks in San Antonio, Texas in 1906, she arrived in Hollywood aged 19. Work in silent pictures soon followed and in 1928 she played a flapper in *Our Dancing Daughters* and emerged a star. She made an easy transition into talkies, her most notable starring roles being in *Mildred Pierce* (1935), *The Women* (1939), and *Johnny Guitar* (1954). She was rarely away from films for long and continued to act until the 1970s.

She perhaps survived, because she adapted physically to changing fashions, without submerging her essential film personality one iota. She always remained a sufferer (whether at the bottom or top of the heap) but a sufferer defiantly facing the future.

Her trademarks were sophistication and independence. Wide shoulders, padded sweaters, severe dresses, all suggested someone able to face anything life threw at her. These outfits suited women, during and after the war, perhaps because some of them were enjoying freedom and independence for the first time. Later, the well-cut sweaters and dresses would be swathed in furs and draped with jewels – but the defiance and independence were still there mesmerizing whole new generations.

Row 1: Sl 1, * K1B, k1, rep. from * to end.
Row 2: Sl 1, k to end.
Row 3: Sl 1, k1, * K1B, k1, rep. from * to last st., k1.
Row 4: Sl 1, k to end.
These 4 rows form the patt.
Continue in patt. until work measures 14¼(13½,13½,13½,13,13,)in / 36(34, 34,34,33,33)cm, ending with a wrong-side row.
Shape armholes
Bind off 4 sts. at beg. of next 2 rows.
Dec. 1 st. each end of every row until 51(51,55,55,57,57)sts. remain. *
Work even until armholes measure 7(7½,7½,7½,8,8)in / 18(19,19,19,20, 20)cm from beg., ending with a wrong-side row.
Shape shoulders
Next row: Bind off 12(12,14,14,15, 15)sts. then patt. across 26 sts., bind off remaining 12(12,14,14,15,15)sts.
Fasten off and leave remaining 27 sts. on a holder.

· FRONT ·

Work as given for back from * to *.
Work even until armholes measure 2¼(3,3,3,3½,3½)in / 6(8,8,8,9,9)cm from beg. of shaping, ending with a wrong-side row.
Shape neck
Next row: Sl 1, patt. 20(20,22,22, 23,23), turn and leave remaining sts. on a spare needle.
Working on the first set of sts. only, continue as follows:
Next row: Sl 1, patt. to last st., k1.
** Dec. 1 st. at neck edge on next and every following alternate row until 12(12,14,14,15,15)sts. remain.
Work even until front measures same as back to shoulders, ending at armhole edge.
Shape shoulder
Bind off. **
Return to remaining sts.

JOAN CRAWFORD
1906–1977

With right side facing, slip first 9 sts. onto a holder, join yarn to next st., then k1, patt. to last st., k1.

Next row: Sl 1, patt. to last st., k1.

Now work as given for first side of neck from ** to **.

· SLEEVES ·

Using size 3 (3¼ mm) needles cast on 56(56,60,60,64,64)sts.

Rep the 2 rib rows 14 times.

Inc. row: Sl 1, p1(1,1,1,3,3), * inc. in next st., p4(4,8,8,8,8), rep. from * to last 4(4,4,4,6,6)sts., inc. in next st., p2(2,2,2,4,4), k1: 67(67,67,67,71,71)sts.

Change to size 5 (4 mm) needles.

K 2 rows.

Proceed in patt as given for back increasing and working into patt 1 st. each end of 3rd and every following 6th(4th,4th,4th,4th,4th)row until there are 77(83,83,83,87,87)sts. Work even until sleeve measures 8¼ in (21 cm), ending with a wrong-side row.

Shape top

Dec. 1 st each end of next and every following 4th row until there are 69(75,75,75,79,79)sts.

Dec. 1 st. at beg. of next 26(32,32,32, 36,36) rows: 43 sts.

Next row: Sl 1, patt to last st., k1.

Bind off.

· NECKBAND ·

Join right shoulder seam.

With right side facing and using size 3 (3¼ mm) needles, pick up and k30 sts. evenly down left side of front neck, k across 9 sts. from front neck holder as follows: k3, [M1, k3] twice, pick up and k30 sts. evenly up right side of front neck then work across 27 sts. from back neck holder as follows: k1, [M1, k5] 5 times, M1, k1: 104 sts.

Beg. rib row 2, work 11 rows in rib.

Bind off loosely in rib.

· FINISHING ·

Join left shoulder and neckband seam. Join side and sleeve seams. Sew in sleeves, forming pleats at top of sleeve to fit. Fold back cuffs.

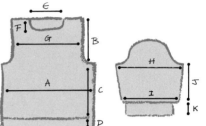

A	17	(18,	19,	19½,	21,	22)	in
	43	(45.5,	48,	50,	53.5,	56)	cm
B	7¼	(7½,	7½,	7½,	7¾,	7¾)	in
	18	(19,	19,	19,	20,	20)	cm
C	11½	(10¾,	10¾,	10¾,	10¼,	10¼)	in
	29	(27,	27,	27,	26,	26)	cm
D	2¾	in					
	7	cm					
E	6¼	in					
	16	cm					
F	4¾	(4¼,	4¼,	4¼,	4¼,	4¼)	in
	12	(11,	11,	11,	11,	11)	cm
G	12	(12,	12½,	12½,	13,	13)	in
	30	(30,	32,	32,	33,	33)	cm
H	17¾	(19½,	19½,	19½,	20,	20)	in
	45	(50,	50,	50,	51,	51)	cm
I	15½	(15½,	15½,	16½,	16½)	in	
	39	(39,	39,	39,	42,	42)	cm
J	4¾	in					
	12	cm					
K	3½	in					
	9	cm					

A figure-hugging turtleneck sweater which is quick to knit. Made in stockinette stitch, it has double-rib bands and collar. The set-in sleeves are given a feminine 1940s look with the help of shoulder pads. For a neat roll neck, the neckband is turned in and slipstitched.

· MEASUREMENTS ·

To fit bust 32(34,36,38)in/81(86,91, 97)cm
Actual measurements 35(36½,38½,40) in/88(92,98,102)cm
Length to shoulders 21½(22,22½,23) in/55(56,57,58)cm
Sleeve seam 17¼(17½,17½,18)in/ 44(45,45,46)cm

· MATERIALS ·

9(9,10,10) × 50g balls Pingouin Escapade
A pair each of size 4 (3¾ mm) and size 6 (4½ mm) knitting needles
Shoulder pads

· GAUGE ·

19 sts. and 24 rows to 4 in (10 cm) over st.st. using size 6 (4½ mm) needles.

· BACK ·

Using size 4 (3¾ mm) needles cast on 68(72,78,82)sts.
Work 16 rows in k2, p2 rib increasing 1 st. each end of last row: 70(74,80, 84)sts.
Change to size 6 (4½ mm) needles.
Beg. k row, work in st.st., inc. 1 st. each end of next and every following 8th row until there are 84(88,94, 98)sts.
Work even until back measures 11(11½,11½,12)in / 27.5(28.5,28.5,

PEGGY CUMMINS
1925 ☞

Miss Cummins was born in Prestatyn, North Wales, but spent her childhood in Killarney, Ireland. In 1938 she came to London to do radio shows and act, and here she was spotted by a 20th Century-Fox talent scout. He saw her as the star of *Forever Amber* (1948) but Hollywood's Linda Darnell won the day, probably because the latter was more established and a bigger box-office pull. Peggy Cummins found herself in her first major Hollywood film *The Late George Apley* (1947) with such distinguished company as Ronald Colman and the spritely Mildred Natwick. In the same year, 1947, she starred opposite Victor Mature in *Moss Rose*, a Victorian melodrama in which she played a lively cockney music hall floosie intent on getting her man and on the way becoming embroiled in murder and intrigue. She returned to England to appear in *Escape* (1948) returning briefly to Hollywood to star in the now respected cult B movie *Gun Crazy* (1950), a savage gangster film and forerunner of *Bonnie and Clyde*.

Thus ended her brief Hollywood career. Competition in Hollywood was tough, and quite a few Celtic beauties, like Maureen O'Hara, Deborah Kerr and Greer Garson were already firmly established there. Maybe Peggy was one too many. With her soft blonde hair and innocent green eyes she was nevertheless an engaging girl whom international success only just eluded. Ironically she is wearing one of the most sensual sweaters in the book: could it be that a potential sex symbol was always lurking underneath?

29.5)cm from beg., ending with a p row.
Shape armholes
Bind off 3 sts. at beg. of next 2 rows.
Dec. 1 st. each end of next 2 rows, then each end of every following alternate row until 68(72,76,80)sts. remain.
Work even until back measures 21½ (22,22½,23)in/55(56,57,58)cm from beg., ending with a p row.
Shape shoulders
Bind off 21(23,24,26)sts. at beg. of next 2 rows.
Break off yarn and leave remaining 26(26,28,28) sts. on a holder.

· FRONT ·

Work as given for back until front measures 18(18½,18½,19)in/46(47, 47,48)cm from beg., ending with a p row.
Shape neck
Next row: K31(33,35,37), turn and leave remaining sts. on a spare needle.
Working on these sts. for first side of neck, dec. 1 st. at neck edge on every row until 23(25,27,29)sts. remain, then on every following alternate row until 21(23,24,26)sts. remain.
Work even until front measures same as back to shoulder, ending with a p row.
Bind off.
Return to remaining sts.
With right side facing, slip first 6 sts. onto a holder, join on yarn and k to end.
Now complete second side of neck to match first, reversing all shaping.

· SLEEVES ·

Using size 4 (3¾ mm) needles cast on 40(40,44,44)sts.
Work 12 rows in k2, p2 rib.
Change to size 6 (4½ mm) needles.
Beg. with a k row, work in st.st. inc. 1 st. each end of next and every follow-

PEGGY CUMMINS
1925 ☞

ing 4th row until there are 50(50,54, 54)sts., then every following 5th row until there are 76(76,80,80)sts.
Work even until sleeve measures 17¼(17½,17½,18)in / 44(45,45,46)cm from beg., ending with a p row.

Shape top
Bind off 3 sts. at beg. of next 4 rows.
Dec. 1 st. each end of every row until 36(36,40,40)sts. remain, then every following alternate row until 30(30, 32,32)sts. remain.
Bind off 4 sts. at beg. of next 4 rows.
Bind off remaining 14(14,16,16)sts.

· NECKBAND ·

Join right shoulder seam.
With right side facing and using size 4 (3¾ mm) needles, pick up and k20(20,23,23)sts. down left side of front neck, k6 sts. from front neck holder, pick up and k20(20,23,23)sts. up right side of front neck, then k26(26,28,28)sts. from back neck holder: 72(72,80,80)sts.
Work 7 in (18 cm) in k2, p2 rib.
Bind off in rib.

· FINISHING ·

Join left shoulder and neckband seam.
Fold sleeves in half lengthwise, then placing folds at top of sleeves to shoulder seams, sew in the sleeves.
Join side and sleeve seams. Sew in shoulder pads. Fold neckband in half to wrong side and slipstitch into place.

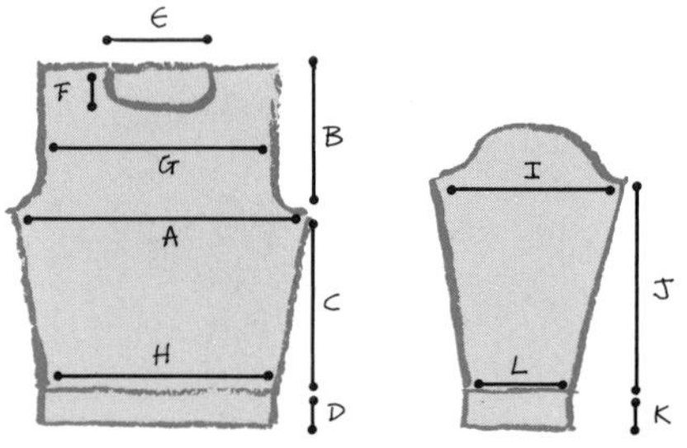

A	17½	(18,	19¼,	20)	in
	44	(46,	49,	51)	cm
B	11	(11,	11¼,	11¼)	in
	27.5	(27.5,	28.5,	28.5)	cm
C	8½	(8¾,	8¾,	9¼)	in
	21.5	(22.5,	22.5,	23.5)	cm
D	2¼				in
	6				cm
E	5½	(5¼,	6,	6)	in
	14	(14,	15,	15)	cm
F	3½	(3½,	4,	4)	in
	9	(9,	10,	10)	cm
G	14	(15,	15¾,	16½)	in
	36	(38,	40,	42)	cm
H	14½	(15½,	16½,	17½)	in
	37	(39,	42,	44)	cm
I	15¾	(15¾,	16½,	16½)	in
	40	(40,	42,	42)	cm
J	15½	(15¾,	15¾,	16)	in
	39	(40,	40,	41)	cm
K	2				in
	5				cm
L	8¼	(8¼,	9,	9)	in
	21	(21,	23,	23)	cm

This man's V-necked sweater with set-in sleeves is worked in a simple variation of garter stitch, and grows quickly in size. The single-rib neckband is worked on a circular needle to avoid a seam.

· MEASUREMENTS ·

To fit chest 36–38(40–42,44–46)in/ 92–97(102–107,112–117)cm
Actual measurements 42½(46,50)in/ 108(117,126)cm
Length to shoulders 24½(25½,26½)in/ 63(65,67)cm
Sleeve seam 18½(19,19¼)in/47(48, 49)cm

· MATERIALS ·

12(13,14) × 50g balls Scheepjeswol Superwash Extra
A pair each of size 2 (3 mm) and size 4 (3¾ mm) knitting needles and one size 2 (3 mm) circular needle 24 in (60 cm) long

· GAUGE ·

18 sts. and 48 rows to 4 in (10 cm) over pattern using size 4 (3¾ mm) needles.

· BACK ·

* Using size 2 (3 mm) needles cast on 97(105,113)sts.
Rib row 1: K1, * p1, k1, rep. from * to end.
Rib row 2: P1, * k1, p1, rep. from * to end.
Rep these 2 rows for 2 in (5 cm), ending with rib row 1.
Change to size 4 (3¾ mm) needles.
K 1 row.
Proceed in patt. as follows:
Row 1: (Right side) K1, * K1B, k1, rep. from * to end.
Row 2: K to end.

ERROL FLYNN

1909-1959

Errol Flynn's very name conjures up the vitality and romance unique to him. Extremely handsome and virile, this hero's youthful adventures made him a suitable candidate for *Boys' Own Annual*; by 24 he had prospected for gold, hunted tropical birds and smuggled diamonds. His appearance as Fletcher Christian in the early Australian film *In the Wake of the Bounty* (1933) prompted a move to England and then to Hollywood, where he soon landed a contract with Warner Brothers. Here he was teamed with another newcomer, Olivia de Havilland, in a series of successful and exciting swashbucklers such as *Captain Blood* (1935), *The Charge of the Light Brigade* (1936) and *The Adventures of Robin Hood* (1938). *The Private Lives of Elizabeth and Essex* (1939) with Bette Davis was also a big success and the public, the press and Hollywood adored him. 1935–1942 were his golden years.

His charming smile, assured gallantry and animal magnetism naturally attracted women on a grand scale and although married to successful actress Lily Damita, Flynn's womanizing and drinking were legendary. But his romantic escapades culminated in a court case for statutory rape, and although he was acquitted, Flynn lost himself in fabled bouts of drinking, and finally died of a heart-attack in Vancouver at age 50.

However, apart from Douglas Fairbanks Snr., no one smiled with such charm, looked so dashing in hose or breeches, or generally swashed a buckle with such an air as Errol Flynn.

Row 3: K2, * K1B, k1, rep. from * to last st., k1.
Row 4: K to end.
These 4 rows form the patt.
Continue in patt. until work measures 16(16½,17)in/41(42,43)cm from beg., ending with a wrong-side row.
Shape armholes
Keeping patt. correct, bind off 4 sts. at beg. of next 2 rows, then 2 sts. at beg. of following 2 rows.
Dec. 1 st. each end of next and every following alternate row until 77(83, 89)sts. remain. *
Work even until armholes measure 8½(9,9½)in/22(23,24)cm from beg. of shaping, ending with a wrong-side row.
Shape shoulders
Bind off 7(8,9)sts. at beg. of next 4 rows, then 8(9,10)sts. at beg. of following 2 rows.
Break off yarn and leave remaining 33 sts. on a holder.

· FRONT ·

Work as given for back from * to *.
Work even until armholes measure 1(1½,2)in/3(4,5)cm from beg. of shaping, ending with a wrong-side row.
Shape neck
Next row: Patt. 38(41,44)sts., turn and leave remaining sts. on a spare needle.
Next row: K to end.
** Dec. 1 st. at neck edge on next and every following 4th row until 22(25, 28)sts. remain.
Work even until front measures same as back to shoulder, ending at armhole edge.
Shape shoulder
Bind off 7(8,9)sts. at beg. of next and following alternate row.
Work 1 row, then bind off. **
Return to remaining sts.
With right side facing, slip first st. onto a safety-pin, rejoin yarn to next

ERROL FLYNN
1909-1959

st., then patt. 2 rows.
Now complete as given for first side of neck from ** to **.

· SLEEVES ·

Using size 2 (3 mm) needles cast on 53(55,57)sts.
Work 3 in (8 cm) in rib as given for back, ending with rib row 1.
Change to size 4 (3¾ mm) needles.
K 1 row.
Proceed in patt. as given for back **at the same time** inc. and work into patt. 1 st. each end of 9th and every following 12th row until there are 79(83,87)sts.
Work even until sleeve measures 18½(19,19¼)in/47(48,49)cm from cast-on edge, ending with a wrong-side row.
Shape top
Bind off 4 sts. at beg. of next 2 rows, then 2 sts. at beg of following 6 rows and 3 sts. at beg. of following 16 rows.
Bind off remaining 11(15,19)sts.

· NECKBAND ·

Join shoulder seams.
With right side facing and using the circular needle, patt. across 33 sts. from back neck holder, pick up and k66 sts. down left side of front neck, k the center st. from safety-pin, then pick up and k66 sts. up right side of front neck: 166 sts.
Round 1: [K1, p1] to within 1 st. of center front st., slip 2 knitwise, k1, pass the 2 slip stitches over, [p1, k1] to end.
Round 2: Rib to within 1 st. of center front st., slip 2 knitwise, k1, pass 2 slip stitches over, rib to end.
Rep. round 2 for 3 cm.
Bind off in rib, decreasing at center front as before.

· FINISHING ·

Fold sleeves in half lengthwise, then placing folds at top of sleeves to shoulder seams, sew into place. Join side and sleeve seams.

A	21¼	(23,	24¾)	in
	54	(58.5,	63)	cm
B	8¾	(9,	9½)	in
	22	(23,	24)	cm
C	14	(14½,	15)	in
	36	(37,	38)	cm
D	2			in
	5			cm
E	7			in
	18			cm
F	7¾			in
	20			cm
G	17½	(18,	19)	in
	44	(46,	48)	cm
H	2			in
	5			cm
I	15½	(15¾,	16)	in
	39	(40,	41)	cm
J	3¼			in
	8			cm
K	11½	(12,	12½)	in
	29.5	(30.5,	31.5)	cm

This sweater has set-in sleeves, round neck and button front opening. The sleeves are finished with button-up cuffs and there are two pockets on the front. It is worked in an unusual hexagon and diamond pattern following the stitch chart. Pocket tops, cuffs, neckband and borders are trimmed with contrast-color stripes.

· MEASUREMENTS ·

To fit bust 34(36,38)in/86(91,97)cm
Actual measurements 38/(39½,42)in/ 96(100,106)cm
Length to shoulders 29½(29½,30)in/ 75(75,76)cm
Sleeve seam 16½ in (42 cm)

· MATERIALS ·

11(12,13) × 50g balls Rowan Classic Tweed in main color A
1 × 50g ball Rowan Designer D.K. in contrast color B
A pair each of size 3 (3¼ mm) and size 5 (4 mm) knitting needles
7 buttons; large shoulder pads

· GAUGE ·

21 sts. and 30 rows to 4 in (10 cm) over pattern using size 5 (4 mm) needles.

· BACK ·

Using size 3 (3¼ mm) needles and A, cast on 101(105,111)sts.
Rib row 1: K1, * p1, k1, rep. from * to end.
Rib row 2: P1, * k1, p1, rep. from * to end.
Rep these 2 rows for 1 in (2.5 cm), ending with a wrong-side row.
Change to size 5 (4 mm) needles.

GRETA GARBO

1905 ☞

If Garbo had been asked to choose what she should wear to be photographed for this book, one feels it could have been this casual sweater and simple hat, a far cry from the clinging velvets and shimmering lamé of her films from the past.

Greta Louisa Gustafsson was born in Stockholm, Sweden, the daughter of a laborer. The young, slightly plump Garbo had worked in a barber shop and modeled hats for a local milliner in Stockholm, when Mauritz Stiller, a notable director at the time, eventually Svengalied her off to Hollywood – but not to immediate fame. Although he was sacked from the silent movie *The Temptress* in which Garbo starred, she went from strength to strength. After much grooming and dieting this magnificent butterfly emerged from the chrysalis. Her love scenes with Hollywood's current heart-throb John Gilbert were unforgettable for their steamy, sensuous passion.

Her flawless appearance and simmering sensuality drained audiences of emotion in several film classics in which she super-starred after a successful transition from silent films to talkies. Her most memorable films were *Queen Christina* (1933), *Camille* (1936) and *Ninotchka* (1939). However, the *Two Faced Woman* (1941) failed at the box office and by chance or accident was Garbo's last ever film. Since the 1940s, she has lived a reclusive life in New York.

Garbo's presence is still felt today in fashion and beauty, and more than 40 years on, le style 'Garbo' has never been matched.

Work the 20 row patt. as given in chart, repeating the 9 st. patt. 11 times and working the 1(3,6) edge sts. as indicated, until back measures 22½ in (57 cm) from beg., ending with a wrong-side row.
Shape armholes
Keeping patt. correct, bind off 3(3, 4)sts. at beg. of next 2 rows, 2(2,3)sts. at beg. of next 2 rows, then 2 sts. at beg. of next 4(4,6) rows.
Dec. 1 st. at beg. of next 4(6,2) rows: 79(81,83)sts.
Work even until back measures 29½ (29½,30)in/75(75,76)cm from beg., ending with a wrong-side row.
Shape shoulders
Bind off 3(4,4)sts. at beg. of next 2 rows and 4 sts. at beg. of following 4 rows.
Shape neck
Next row: Bind off 4 sts. patt until there are 20(20,21)sts. on the needle, bind off 9 sts., patt. to end.
Work on first set of sts. as follows:
Next row: Bind off 4 sts., patt. to end.
Next row: Bind off 6 sts., patt. to end.
Rep. these 2 rows once more.
Bind off remaining 4(4,5)sts.
Return to remaining sts.
With wrong side facing, rejoin yarn to remaining sts., bind off 6 sts., patt. to end.
Next row: Bind off 4 sts., patt. to end.
Next row: Bind off 6 sts., patt. to end.
Bind off remaining 4(4,5)sts.

· POCKET LININGS ·

MAKE 2

Using size 5 (4 mm) needles and A bind on 28 sts.
Work 3 in (8 cm) st.st., ending with a p row.
Break off yarn and leave sts. on a spare needle.

· FRONT ·

Work as given for back until front measures 4¼ in (11 cm) from beg.,

GRETA GARBO
1905 ☞

ending with a wrong-side row.

Place pockets

Next row: Patt. 10(12,15)sts., slip next 28 sts. onto a holder and in their place patt. across sts. of first pocket lining, patt. 25 sts., slip next 28 sts. onto a holder and in their place patt. across sts. of second pocket lining, patt. to end.

Continue in patt. until work measures 20 in (51 cm) from beg., ending with a wrong-side row.

Divide for front opening

Next row: Patt. 47(49,52)sts., bind off next 7 sts., patt. to end.

Work on first side of neck as follows:

Keeping patt. correct, work even until front measures same as back to beg. of armhole shaping, ending at armhole edge.

Shape armhole

Bind off 3(3,4)sts. at beg. of next row, 2(2,3)sts. at beg. of following alternate row, then 2 sts. at beg. of following 2(2,3) alternate rows.

Dec. 1 st. at armhole edge at beg. of following 2(3,2) alternate rows: 36(37,38)sts.

Work even until the front measures 11 rows less than back to beg. of shoulder shaping, ending at neck edge.

Shape neck

Bind off 3 sts. at beg. of next row, then 2 sts. at beg. of following 3 alternate rows.

Dec. 1 st. at neck edge at beg. of following 2 alternate rows, so ending at armhole edge.

Shape shoulder

Next row: Bind off 3(4,4)sts., patt. to end.

Next row: Work 2 tog., patt. to end.

Next row: Bind off 4 sts., patt. to end.

Next row: Work 2 tog., patt. to end.

Bind off 4 sts. at beg. of next and following 2 alternate rows.

Work 1 row.

Bind off remaining 4(4,5)sts.

Return to remaining sts.

With wrong side facing, join on A and patt. to end.

Now complete to match first side of neck, reversing all shaping.

· RIGHT SLEEVE ·

First half of cuff: Using size 3 (3¼ mm) needles and A, cast on 28(28, 31)sts.

P 2 rows, k 1 row, p 1 row, then k 2 rows.

Join in B.

Next row: With B, * k1, sl 1 pw., rep. from * to last st., k1.

Next row: With B, * k1, ytf., sl 1 pw., ytb., rep. from * to last st., k1.

With A, k 3 rows, p 1 row, then k 2 rows.

Next row: With B, * k1, sl 1 pw., rep. from * to last st., k1.

Next row: With B, * k1, ytf., sl 1 pw., ytb., rep. from * to last st., k1.

Break off B.

With A, k 3 rows, p 1 row, then k 1 row.

Break off yarn and leave sts. on a spare needle.

Second half of cuff: Using size 3 (3¼ mm) needles and A, cast on 24(24, 27)sts. and work as given for first half of cuff but do not break off yarn.

Next row: (Wrong side) K19(19,22) of second cuff, then holding the 5 remaining sts. of second cuff in front of the first 5 sts. of first cuff, k tog. 1 st. from each needle five times, k remaining 22(22,26)sts: 47(47,53)sts.

Change to size 5 (4 mm) needles.

Work in patt. from chart, increasing and working into patt. 1 st. each end of 5th and every following 6th row until there are 81(81,67)sts., then **for 3rd size only** inc. 1 st. at each end of every following 7th row until there are 85 sts.

Work even until sleeve measures 16½ in (42 cm) from beg., ending with a wrong-side row.

Shape top

Bind off 3 sts. at beg. of next 2 rows and 2 sts. at beg. of following 8(8,12) rows.

Dec. 1 st. at beg. of next 34(34,30) rows.

Bind off 2 sts. at beg. of next 2 rows and 3 sts. at beg. of following 2 rows.

Bind off remaining 15 sts.

· LEFT SLEEVE ·

Work as given for right sleeve except work second half of cuff first, break off yarn, then do not break off yarn after working first half.

Join cuff sections as follows:

Next row: (Wrong side) K22(22,26) of section just worked, then holding the 5 remaining sts. of this cuff in front of the first 5 sts. of second piece of cuff, k tog. 1 st. from each needle five times, k remaining 19(19,22)sts: 47(47,53)sts.

Complete as given for right sleeve.

· NECKBAND ·

Join shoulder seams.

With right side facing, using size 3 (3¼ mm) needles and A, pick up and k26 sts. up right side of front neck, 39 sts. across back neck, then 26 sts. down left side of front neck: 91 sts.

* P 1 row and k 2 rows.

Next row: With B * k1, sl 1 pw., rep. from * to last st., k1.

Next row: With B, * k1, ytf., sl 1 pw., ytb., rep. from * to last st., k1.

Break off B.

With A, K 3 rows, p 1 row, k 1 row, then p 3 rows.

Beg. with a k row, work 10 rows st.st.

Bind off loosely.

Fold band in half to wrong side and slipstitch into position. *

· FRONT BANDS ·

BOTH ALIKE

With right side facing, using size 3 (3¼ mm) needles and A, pick up and

k49 sts. evenly along front neck opening and neckband edge.
Work as given for neckband from * to *

Lap right band over left and neatly slipstitch lower edges into position.

· POCKET TOPS ·

With right side facing, slip 28 sts. from holder onto a size 3 (3¼ mm) needle, join on yarn and cast on 1 st: 29 sts.
Now work band as given for neckband from * to *.

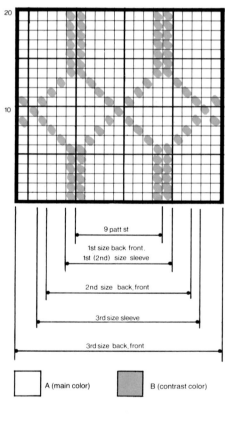

| | | 9 patt st | | |

1st size back front.
1st (2nd) size sleeve

2nd size back, front

3rd size sleeve

3rd size back, front

☐ A (main color)   ▨ B (contrast color)

· CUFF EDGING ·

With right side of cuff facing, using size 3 (3¼ mm) needles and A, pick up and k12 sts. along outer edge of cuff opening.
K 2 rows.
Bind off knitwise.

· FINISHING ·

Work a button loop at lower edge of each outer cuff edging, sew on button

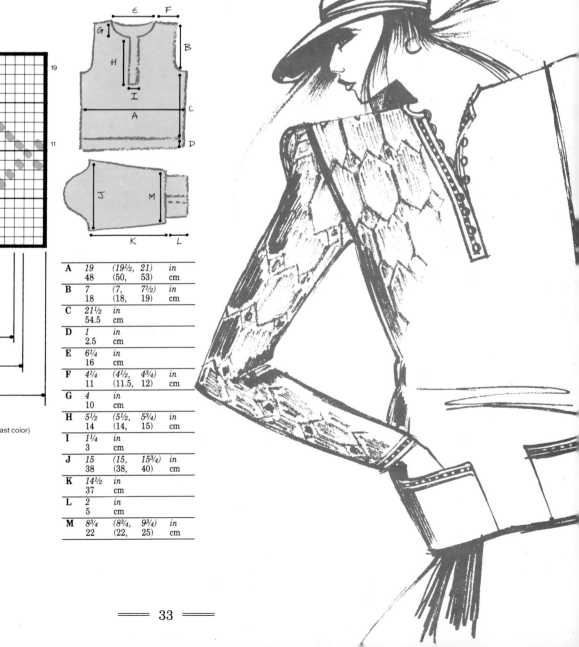

A	19 48	(19½, (50,	21) 53)	in cm
B	7 18	(7, (18,	7½) 19)	in cm
C	21½ 54.5			in cm
D	1 2.5			in cm
E	6¼ 16			in cm
F	4¼ 11	(4½, (11.5,	4¾) 12)	in cm
G	4 10			in cm
H	5½ 14	(5½, (14,	5¾) 15)	in cm
I	1¼ 3			in cm
J	15 38	(15, (38,	15¾) 40)	in cm
K	14½ 37			in cm
L	2 5			in cm
M	8¾ 22	(8¾, (22,	9¾) 25)	in cm

on inner cuff edge to correspond with button loop. Work 5 button loops on right front edge, the first at top of neckband, the next 1 in (3 cm) from lower edge of neck opening and the rest evenly spaced.
Sew on the buttons to correspond with button loops. Sew down pocket linings, then sew down side edges of pocket tops. Sew in sleeves. Join side and sleeve seams. Sew in shoulder pads.

Cuddly angora and cool cotton combine to make this unusual stockinette-stitch cardigan with short puffed sleeves. The button borders and sleeves are made in angora with the back and fronts knitted in cotton. Pretty embroidered flowers in lazy daisy and satin stitch with French knots complete the picture.

· MEASUREMENTS ·

To fit bust 32(34,36,38)in/81(86,91, 97)cm
Actual measurements 35(37¼,39, 41)in/89(94,99,104)cm
Length to shoulders 18½(19,19)in/ 47(47,48,48)cm
Sleeve seam 4 in (10 cm)

· MATERIALS ·

4(4,5,5) × 50g balls Georges Picaud Cotton Club
10(10,11,11) × 10g balls Georges Picaud 100% Angora
A pair each of size 5 (4 mm) and size 6 (4½ mm) knitting needles
Colored thread for embroidering flowers
8 buttons

· GAUGE ·

24 sts. and 30 rows to 4 in (10 cm) over st.st. using size 6 (4½ mm) needles.

· BACK ·

Using size 5 (4 mm) needles and cotton, cast on 85(89,95,99)sts.
Rib row 1: K1, * p1, k1, rep. from * to end.
Rib row 2: P1, * k1, p1, rep. from * to end.

JUDY GARLAND

1922-1969

Judy Garland, born Frances Gumm, was destined to be a legend. Largely encouraged by her mother who was in Vaudeville, Judy began her career at the age of three but from the beginning she was subjected to strict routine, prescribed diets and early calls. This probably accounted for her nervous disposition, but it was this very vulnerability which ignited the famous Judy Garland flame that held audiences spellbound all over the world. With her truly remarkable singing voice she could melt the hardest heart.

She made her first film in 1936 and in 1939 was cast as Dorothy in *The Wizard of Oz*. Garland made history. 'Over the Rainbow' became *her* song. Her follow up films including *Babes in Arms* (1940) and *Strike up the Band* (1940), both with Mickey Rooney, were also hits and her success was unquestionable. In *Meet me in St. Louis* (1944), directed by Vincent Minnelli, later to become her second husband, Judy beat all box office expectations making the film the highest grossing movie musical up to that time. What could go wrong?

Sadly by the time she completed *A Star is Born* (1954), Garland had begun to burn herself out. Her increasing reliance on pills for zest took its toll, film offers dried up and in 1969 she died of an accidental overdose.

A perpetual Peter Pan with her innocent looks, Judy Garland never had an ideal figure and her weight fluctuated wildly, but on screen she always looked flawless. She remains one of Hollywood's best loved stars.

Rep these 2 rows for 1½ in (4 cm), ending rib row 1.
Inc row: Rib 6(4,8,6), * M1, rib 4, rep. from * to last 7(5,7,5)sts., M1, rib to end: 104(110,116,122)sts.
Change to size 6 (4½ mm) needles.
Proceed in st.st. until back measures 10½(10½,10¾,10¾)in / 27(27,28,28) cm from beg., ending with a p row.

Shape armholes
Bind off 6 sts. at beg. of next 2 rows.
Dec. 1 st. each end of every row until 88(88,90,90)sts. remain.
Work even until armholes measure 8(8,8½,8½)in / 20(20,22,22)cm from beg., ending with a p row.
Shape shoulders
Bind off 16 sts. at beg. of next 4 rows.
Break off yarn and leave remaining 24(24,26,26)sts. on a holder.

· LEFT FRONT ·

* Using size 5 (4 mm) needles and cotton, cast on 43(45,47,49)sts.
Work the 2 rib rows for 1½ in (4 cm), ending rib row 1.
Inc. row: Rib 6(4,4,2), * M1, rib 4, rep. from * to last 5(5,3,3)sts., M1, rib to end: 52(55,58,61)sts. *
Change to size 6 (4½ mm) needles.
Proceed in st.st. until work measures same as back to armhole, ending with a p row.
Shape armhole
Bind off 6 sts. at beg. of next row.
Work 1 row even.
Dec. 1 st. at armhole edge on every row until 44(44,45,45)sts. remain.
Work even until armhole measures 4¼(4¼,5,5)in / 11(11,13,13)cm from beg., ending at front edge.
Shape neck
Bind off 6 sts. at beg. of next row.
Dec. 1 st. at neck edge on next and every following alternate row until 32 sts. remain.
Work even until front measures same

as back to shoulder, ending at armhole edge.
Shape shoulder
Bind off 16 sts. at beg. of next row.
Work 1 row. Bind off.

· RIGHT FRONT ·

Work as given for left front from * to *.
Change to size 6 (4½ mm) needles.
Proceed in st.st. until work measures same as back to armhole, ending with a k row.
Now complete as given for left front, reversing all shaping.

· SLEEVES ·

Using size 5 (4 mm) needles and angora, cast on 49(49,51,51)sts.
Work the 2 rib rows for 1 in (3 cm), ending rib row 1.
Inc. row: Rib 4(4,2,2), * M1, rib 2, rep. from * to last 3 sts., M1, rib to end: 71(71,75,75)sts.
Change to size 6 (4½ mm) needles.
Proceed in st.st. until work measures 5 in (13 cm) from beg., ending with a p row.
Shape top
Bind off 6 sts. at beg. of next 2 rows.
Dec. 1 st. at beg. of every row until 51 sts. remain.
Work even until sleeve measures 10(10,10½,10½)in / 25(25,27,27)cm from beg., ending with a p row.
Bind off.

· NECKBAND ·

Join shoulder seams.
With right side facing, using size 5 (4 mm) needles and angora, pick up and k23 sts. up right front neck, k across 24(24,26,26)sts. from back neck holder, then pick up and k24 sts. down left front neck: 71(71,73,73)sts.
Beg. rib row 2, work 5 rows in rib.
Bind off in rib.

· BUTTON BORDER ·

Using size 5 (4 mm) needles and angora, cast on 7 sts.
Rib row 1: (Right side) K2, * p1, k1, rep. from * to last st., k1.
Rib row 2: K1, * p1, k1, rep. from * to end.
Rep. these 2 rows until border, slightly stretched, fits up front to top of neckband.
Sew on the border, then mark positions for 8 buttons, the first one ½ in (1.5 cm) from cast-on edge, the top one ½ in (1.5 cm) from bind-off edge and the others spaced evenly in between.

· BUTTONHOLE BORDER ·

Work as given for button border, working buttonholes to correspond with markers as follows:
Buttonhole row: (Right side) K2, p1, yrn, p2 tog., k2.

· FINISHING ·

Sew on buttonhole border. Join side and sleeve seams. Sew in sleeves, forming gathers at top of sleeve to fit. Sew on buttons.
Using lazy daisy stitch for the leaves and satin stitch and French knots for flowers, embroider sprays of flowers as shown in illustration.

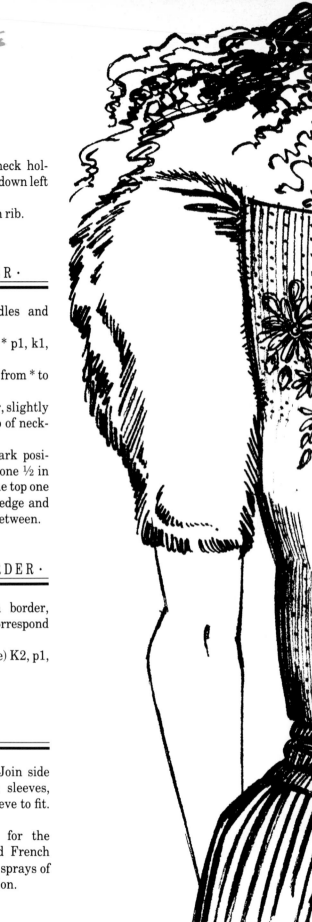

A	17	(18,	19,	20)	in
	43	(46,	48,	51)	cm
B	7¾	(7¾,	8¾,	8¾)	in
	20	(20,	22,	22)	cm
C	9	(9,	9½,	9½)	in
	23	(23,	24,	24)	cm
D	1½				in
	4				cm
E	5¼				in
	13				cm
F	4	(4,	4¼,	4¼)	in
	10	(10,	11,	11)	cm
G	3½				in
	9				cm
H	8½	(9,	9½,	10)	in
	21.5	(23,	24,	25.5)	cm
I	12	(12,	12¼,	12¼)	in
	30	(30,	31,	31)	cm
J	4¾	(4¾,	5½,	5½)	in
	12	(12,	14,	14)	cm
K	4				in
	10				cm
L	1¼				in
	3				cm
M	8¼				in
	21				cm

This cricket-style sweater with bold contrast stripes at neck, cuffs and waist is knitted in cotton. The ribbing is worked in double rib while the back, front and sleeves are knitted in panels of cable and stockinette stitch. Choose white or cream and add your own contrast colors.

· MEASUREMENTS ·

To fit chest 36(38–40,42–44)in/91 (97–102,107–112)cm
Actual measurements 44(48,52)in/ 112(122,132)cm
Length to shoulders 27(27½,28)in/ 69(70,71)cm
Sleeve seam 21½(22,22½)in/55(56, 57)cm

· MATERIALS ·

14(15,16) × 50g balls Pingouin Coton Naturel 8 in main color A
2 balls same in contrast color B
1 ball same in contrast color C
A pair each of size 3 (3¼ mm) and size 5 (4 mm) knitting needles

· GAUGE ·

20 sts. and 26 rows to 4 in (10 cm) over st.st. using size 5 (4 mm) needles.

· SPECIAL ABBREVIATION ·

C8F., Cable 8 Front as follows: slip next 4 sts. onto cable needle and leave at front of work, k4, then k4 from cable needle.

· NOTE ·

When using several colors in one row, use a separate small ball of yarn for each area of color, and twist yarns together on wrong side of work when changing color to avoid making a hole.

CARY GRANT
1904–1986

Mae West always claimed that she discovered Cary Grant and although he had made earlier films, it did his career no harm to appear in movies with the blatantly sexy Mae. One of the most popular actors ever to grace the screen, to his vast array of fans he was the embodiment of health, casual elegance and boyish charm. Such films as *Bringing Up Baby* (1938) with Katharine Hepburn and *The Awful Truth* (1937) with Irene Dunne saw Grant excel as an actor of considerable skill in a combination of sophisticated slapstick and pure romance.

Later, with Alfred Hitchcock, he added another dimension to his expertise, by portraying a callous schemer in *Suspicion* (1941) with co-star Joan Fontaine. His long association with Hitchcock produced some of his most memorable movies, notably *To Catch a Thief* (1955) with Grace Kelly and *North by Northwest* (1959) co-starring Eva Marie Saint. Cary Grant was one of Hitchcock's favorite leading men since he was a perfect foil for the typical cool Aryan blondes preferred by this masterly director.

In his private life, Grant had an air of restlessness, with four marriages ending quickly in divorce, though his fifth and last was long and happy. Later he was content to abandon the silver screen for the world of big business, and became a very rich man – quite an achievement for the young Archibald Leach, as he was christened 83 years ago in Bristol. Nevertheless, he will always be remembered for le style 'sporty' and the clean cut suits which labeled him as one of the most dapper actors ever to grace the screen.

· BACK ·

Using size 3 (3¼ mm) needles and A, cast on 108(116,124)sts.
Work 3½ in (9 cm) in k2, p2 rib, ending with a right-side row.
Inc. row: Rib 14(9,8), * M1, rib 16(14,12), rep. from * to last 14(9,8)sts, M1, rib to end: 114(124,134)sts.
Change to size 5 (4 mm) needles.
Join on and cut off colors as necessary.
Using B and beg. with a k row, work 10 rows st.st.
Inc. row: Using A, k12(14,17), * M1, k18(19,20), rep. from * to last 12(15, 17)sts., M1, k to end: 120(130, 140)sts.
Foundation row: (Wrong side) Using A, p14(19,24), [k2, p8] 9 times, k2, p14(19,24).
Continuing in A, work in patt. as follows:
Row 1: K14(19,24), p2, [k8, p2] 9 times, k14(19,24).
Row 2: P14(19,24), [k2, p8] 9 times, k2, p14(19,24).
Row 3: K14(19,24), p2, [C8F., p2, k8, p2) 4 times, C8F., p2, k14(19,24).
Row 4: As row 2.
Rows 5 to 10: Rep. rows 1 and 2 three times.
These 10 rows form patt.
Continue in patt. until work measures 25½(26,26½)in/65(66,67)cm from beg., ending with a wrong-side row.
Set position for colored stripes at neck as follows:
Next row: Patt. 40(45,50)A, k40B, with A patt. to end.
Next row: Patt. 39(44,49)A, p42B, with A patt. to end.
Continue in this way, working 1 st. less each side in A and 2 more sts. in B, for 4 more rows.
Next row: Patt.35(40,45)A, k5B, k40C, k5B, patt.35(40,45)A.
Next row: Patt.34(39,44)A, p5B, p42C, p5B, patt.34(39,44)A.
Next row: Patt.34(39,44)A, k5B, k42C, k5B, patt.34(39,44)A.

CARY GRANT
1904–1986

A	22	(24,	26)	in
	56	(61,	66)	cm
B	23½	(24,	24½)	in
	60	(61,	62)	cm
C	3½			in
	9			cm
D	6¾			in
	17			cm
E	9¾			in
	25			cm
F	21¼	(22,	22½)	in
	54	(56,	57)	cm
G	11½	(12¼,	12¼)	in
	29	(31,	31)	cm
H	17	(17½,·	17¾)	in
	43	(44,	45)	cm
I	4¾			in
	12			cm

Next row: Patt.33(38,43)A, p5B, p44C, p5B, patt.33(38,43)A.

Shape shoulders

Keeping colors and patt. as set, bind off 21(24,27)sts. at beg. of next 2 rows, then 22(24,26)sts. at beg. of following 2 rows.

Break off yarn and leave remaining 34 sts. on a holder.

· FRONT ·

Work as given for back until front measures 14½(15,15¼)in/37(38,39)cm from beg., ending with wrong-side row. Now set colors for neck stripes as follows:

Next row: Patt.59(64,69)A, k2B, patt.59(64,69)A.

Next row: Patt.59(64,69)A, p2B, patt.59(64,69)A.

Next row: Patt.58(63,68)A, k4B, patt.58(63,69)A.

Next row: Patt.58(63,68)A, p.4B, patt.58(63,68)A.

Continue in this way, working 1 st. less each side in A and 2 sts. more in B on every alternate row until the row with p10B in center has been worked.

Next row: Patt.54(59,64)A, k5B, k2C, k5B, patt.54(59,64)A.

Next row: Patt.54(59,64)A, p5B, p2C, p5B, patt.54(59,64)A.

Continue in this way, working 1 st. less each side in A and 2 sts. more in C on every alternate row until the row with p10C in center has been worked.

Divide for neck

Next row: Patt. 49(54,59)A, k5B, k4C, using C k2 tog., turn and leave remaining sts. on a spare needle.

Next row: P5C, p5B, patt.49(54,59)A.

Next row: Patt.48(53,58)A, k5B, k4C, using C work 2 tog.

Next row: P5C, p5B, patt.48(53,58)A.

Continue in this way, working 1 st. less in A and working 2 tog. in C on every alternate row until 43(48,53)sts.

remain.

Work even in colors and patt. as set until front measures same as back to shoulder, ending at armhole edge.

Shape shoulder

Bind off 21(24,27)sts. at beg. of next row.

Work 1 row, then bind off.

Return to remaining sts.

With right side facing, join on C and k2 tog., k4C, k5B, patt.49(54,59)A.

Next row: Patt.49(54,59)A, p5B, p5C.

Now complete to match first side of neck, reversing all shaping.

· SLEEVES ·

Using size 3 (3¼ mm) needles and A, cast on 56(60,60)sts.

Work 4¾ in (12 cm) k2, p2 rib, increasing 1 st. each end of last row: 58(62,62)sts.

Change to size 5 (4 mm) needles.

Using B and beg. k row, work 6 rows st.st. increasing 1 st. each end of first and 3rd row: 62(66,66)sts.

Using C, work 6 rows st.st. increasing 1 st. each end of first and 3rd row: 66(70,70)sts.

Now continuing in A only and inc. 1 st. each end, work 1 row st.st.: 68(72, 72)sts.

Foundation row: P8(10,10)sts., [k2, p8] 5 times, k2, p8(10,10).

Now work in patt. as follows:

Row 1: K8(10,10)sts., [p2, C8F., p2, k8] twice, p2, C8F., p2, k8(10,10).

Row 2: P8(10,10)sts., [k2, p8] 5 times, k2, p8(10,10).

Row 3: Inc. in first st., k7(9,9), p2, [k8, p2] 5 times, k7(9,9), inc. in last st.

Row 4: P9(11,11)sts., [k2, p8] 5 times, k2, p9(11,11).

Row 5: K9(11,11), p2, [k8, p2] 5 times, k9(11,11).

Row 6: As row 4.

Row 7: Inc. in first st., k8(10,10), p2, [k8, p2] 5 times, k8(10,10), inc. in last st.

Row 8: P10(12,12)sts., [k2, p8] 5 times, k2, p10(12,12).

Row 9: K10(12,12), p2, [k8, p2] 5 times, k10(12,12).

Row 10: As row 8.

Continue in patt. increasing and working into st.st. 1 st. each end of next and every following 4th row until there are 108(112,114)sts.

Work even until sleeve measures 55(56,57)sts. from beg., ending with a wrong-side row.

Bind off.

· NECKBAND ·

Join right shoulder seam, taking care to match stripes.

With right side facing and using size 3 (3¼ mm) needles and A, pick up and k52 sts. down left side of front neck, pick up loop between sts. at center of 'V' and k into back of it, then mark this st. with a colored thread to denote center st., pick up and k52 sts up right side of front neck, then k across 34 sts. from back neck holder: 139 sts.

Rib row 1: [P2, k2] to within 2 sts. of center st., p2 tog., p center st., p2 tog., [k2, p2] to end.

Rib row 2: Rib to within 2 sts. of center st., p2 tog., k center st., p2 tog., rib to end.

Rep. these 2 rows twice more.

Bind off in rib, decreasing each side of center st. as before.

· FINISHING ·

Join left shoulder and neckband seam, matching stripes on shoulder.

Place markers approximately 10½(11, 11½)in/27(28,29)cm below shoulder seams on back and front to denote beg. of armholes. Sew in sleeves between markers, then, matching stripes, join side and sleeve seams.

This sophisticated cotton cardigan with short sleeves and a V-neck is worked in stockinette stitch with a ribbed yoke. The collar and button borders are worked in horizontal rib using a circular needle. Shoulder pads give the cardigan an elegant line – ideal for teaming with a slimline skirt.

· MEASUREMENTS ·

To fit bust 32(34,36,38,40)in / 81(86, 91,97,102)cm
Actual measurements 34(36,38,40, 42)in/86(91,97,102,107)cm
Length to shoulders 22(22½,23, 23¼,23½)in/56(57,58,59,60)cm
Sleeve seam 6¼ in (16 cm)

· MATERIALS ·

6(6,7,7,8) × 50g balls Galler Lino Fino
A pair each of size 1 (2¾ mm) and size 4 (3¾ mm) knitting needles
One size 1 (2¾ mm) circular knitting needle 40 in (100cm) long
5 buttons; shoulder pads

· GAUGE ·

24 sts. and 32 rows to 4 in (10 cm) measured over st.st. using size 4 (3¾ mm) needles.

· BACK ·

Using size 1 (2¾ mm) needles cast on 99(105,111,117,123)sts.
Rib row 1: K1, * p1, k1, rep. from * to end.
Rib row 2: P1, * k1, p1, rep. from * to end.
Rep these 2 rows for 2 in (5 cm), ending with rib row 1.
Inc. row: Rib 20(22,22,22,26), * M1,

JANE GREER

1924 ☞

Hollywood needed villainesses as well as heroines and Bettejane Greer, as Jane Greer was born, seemed to fit the bill to perfection. Pushed by an ambitious, stage-struck mother, Bettejane was modeling professionally at 12, and later worked as a vocalist, singing Latin-American numbers in a Washington night club.

During one of her modeling assignments she caught the attention of the elusive Howard Hughes who put her under contract, but after a year no suitable roles had been found for her. In 1943, she married crooner Rudy Vallee who secured her a contract with RKO studios. The marriage was short-lived but her career took an upswing. She soon graduated from B movies to more prestigious roles, often still cast as the villainess but excelling as the classic *femme fatale*. One of the most notable of her films was *Out of the Past* (1947) with Robert Mitchum. In the 1952 version of *The Prisoner of Zenda* with Stewart Granger and Deborah Kerr, she played Black Prince Michael's (Robert Douglas) love interest, coming to a sticky end. She looked beautiful in the film, her dark and romantic appearance providing a perfect foil for Miss Kerr's English rose.

From leopard skin print dresses to 'sassy' period costumes, she always had style and flair. Her modeling experience gave her poise and a natural ease, enabling her to show off a garment to its best advantage. However, Jane Greer, as she was known in films, was not a wildly ambitious woman and she chose to semi-retire from the screen in 1953 to raise a family returning occasionally to the screen.

rib 20(20,22,24,24), rep. from * to last 19(23,23,23,25)sts., M1, rib to end: 103(109,115,121,127)sts.
Change to size 4 (3¾ mm) needles.
Beg. with a k row, work in st.st. until back measures 14¼ in (36 cm) from beg., ending with a k row.
Next row: P1, * k1, p1, rep. from * to end.
Shape armholes
Keeping rib patt. correct, bind off 4 sts. at beg. of next 2 rows.
Dec. 1 st. each end of next and every following alternate row until 85(89, 93,97,101)sts. remain.
Work even until armholes measure 8(8¼,8½,9,9½)in / 20(21,22,23,24)cm from beg., ending with a wrong-side row.
Shape shoulders
Bind off 8(8,9,9,10)sts. at beg. of next 4 rows, then 8(9,9,10,10)sts. at beg. of next 2 rows.
Break off yarn and leave remaining 37(39,39,41,41)sts. on a holder.

· LEFT FRONT ·

Using size 1 (2¾ mm) needles cast on 44(48,50,54,56)sts.
Work 2 in (5 cm) in k1, p1 rib, ending with a right-side row.
Inc. row: Rib 12(12,14,14,14), * M1, rib 11(24,12,26,14), rep. from * to last 10(12,12,14,14)sts., M1, rib to end: 47(50,53,56,59)sts.
Change to size 4 (3¾ mm) needles.
Beg. with a k row, work in st.st. until front measures 6 rows less than back to beg. of armhole shaping.
Shape front edge
Next row: K to last 3 sts., k2 tog., k1.
Work 3 rows straight.
Next row: K to last 3 sts., k2 tog., k1.
Next row: P1(0,1,0,1), [k1, p1] to end.
Continuing in rib as now set, shape armhole and front edge as follows:
Row 1: Bind off 4 sts., rib to end.
Row 2: Rib to end.

Row 3: Work 2 tog., rib to last 2 sts., work 2 tog.
Row 4: Rib to end.
Row 5: Work 2 tog., rib to end.
Row 6: Rib to end.
Rep. rows 3 to 6 until 33(35,36,38, 39)sts. remain, ending with row 4(6,4, 6,4).
Keeping armhole edge straight, continue to dec. at front edge until 24(25,27,28,30)sts. remain.
Work even until armhole measures same as back to shoulder, ending at armhole edge.
Shape shoulder
Bind off 8(8,9,9,10)sts. at beg. of next and following alternate row.
Work 1 row, then bind off.

· RIGHT FRONT ·

Work as given for left front, reversing all shapings.

· SLEEVES ·

Using size 1 (2¾ mm) needles cast on 71(71,73,73,75)sts.
Work the 2 rib rows for 1½ in (4 cm), ending rib row 2.
Change to size 4 (3¾ mm) needles.
Continuing in rib, inc. 1 st. each end of next and every following 3rd row taking inc. sts. into rib, until there are 83(87,91,95,99)sts.
Work even until sleeve measures 6½ in (16 cm) from beg., ending with a wrong-side row.
Shape top
Bind off 4 sts. in rib at beg. of next 2 rows.
Dec. 1 st. each end of next and every following 4th row until 57(61,65,69, 73)sts. remain, then every following alternate row until 55 sts. remain, ending with a wrong-side row.
Bind off 2 sts. in rib at beg. of next 4 rows, 4 sts. at beg. of next 4 rows, then 6 sts. at beg. of next 2 rows.
Bind off remaining 19 sts.

· FRONT BORDER AND COLLAR ·

Join shoulder seams.
With right side facing and using size 1 (2¾ mm) circular needle, pick up and k95 sts. evenly up right front to beg. of front edge shaping and 63(65,69,71, 75)sts up neck edge to shoulder, k across back neck sts. from holder as follows: rib 5(6,6,6,6), [M1, rib 4]7 times, M1, rib 4(5,5,7,7), then pick up and k63(65,69,71,75)sts. evenly down left front neck to beg. of shaping and 95 sts. down left front to lower edge: 361(367,375,381,389)sts.
Beg. rib row 2, work 4 rows in rib.
Shape collar
Next row: Rib 260(266,274,280,288), turn.
Next row: Sl 1, rib 158(164,172,178, 186), turn.
Next row: Sl 1, rib 152(158,166,172, 180), turn.
Continue in this way, working 6 sts. less on every row, until 24 rows have been worked from beg. of shaping.
Next row: Sl 1, rib to end.
Next row: Rib to end.
Next row: Rib to last 85 sts., bind off 2 sts., [rib 18, bind off 2 sts.] 4 times, rib to end.
Next row: Rib to end, casting on 2 sts. over those bind off in previous row.
Work 6 rows in rib.
Bind off loosely in rib.

· FINISHING ·

Do not press. Sew in sleeves, Join side and sleeve seams. Sew on buttons.
Sew in shoulder pads.

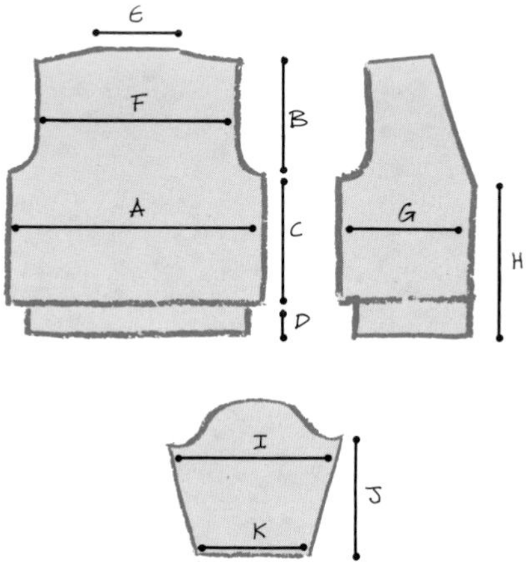

A	*17*	(18,	19,	20,	21)	in
	43	(45.5,	48,	51,	53)	cm
B	*7¾*	*(8¼,*	*8¾,*	*9,*	*9½)*	*in*
	20	(21,	22,	23,	24)	cm
C	*12¼*	*in*				
	31	cm				
D	*2*	*in*				
	5	cm				
E	*6*	*(6¼,*	*6¼,*	*6¾,*	*6¾)*	*in*
	15	(16,	16,	17,	17)	cm
F	*13¾*	*(14½,*	*15,*	*15¾,*	*16¼)*	*in*
	35	(37,	38,	40,	42)	cm
G	*7¾*	*(8¼,*	*8¾,*	*9,*	*9½)*	*in*
	19.5	(21,	22,	23,	24)	cm
H	*13½*	*in*				
	34	cm				
I	*13½*	*(14,*	*14½,*	*15½,*	*16)*	*in*
	34	(36,	37,	39,	41)	cm
J	*6¼*	*in*				
	16	cm				
K	*11½*	*(11½,*	*12,*	*12,*	*12¼)*	*in*
	29	(29,	30,	30,	31)	cm

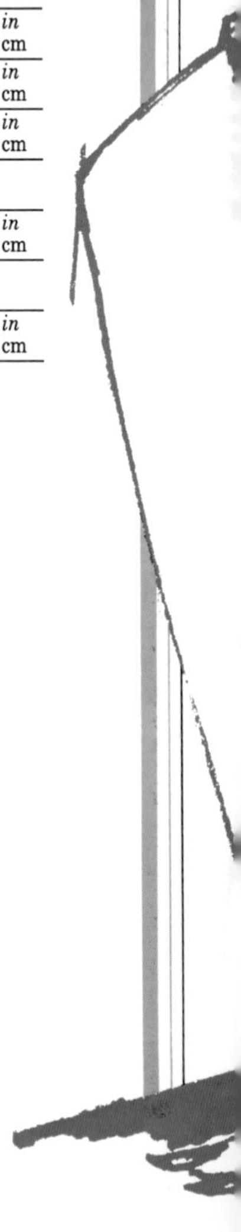

This button-fronted sweater with collar has set-in sleeves in a choice of lengths. Both versions, long or short-sleeved, have double-rib cuffs to match the ribbing at the waist; the single-rib collar is knitted separately.

· MEASUREMENTS ·

To fit bust 32(34,36,38)in/81(86,91, 97)cm
Actual measurements 38(40¼,42½, 45) in/96(102,108,114)cm
Length to shoulders 22½(23,23¼, 23½)in/57(58,59,60)cm
Sleeve seam – short 4 in (10 cm)
Sleeve seam – long 16½(17,17¼, 17½)in/42(43,44,45)cm

· MATERIALS ·

Short sleeved version:
7(7,8,8) × 40g balls Phildar Phil-'Douce
Long sleeved version:
8(9,9,10) × 40g balls Phildar Phil-'Douce
A pair each of size 1 (2¾ mm), size 2 (3 mm) and size 4 (3¾ mm) knitting needles; 5 buttons

· GAUGE ·

22 sts. and 31 rows to 4 in (10 cm) over st.st. using size 4 (3¾ mm) needles.

· BACK ·

Using size 1 (2¾ mm) needles cast on 100(106,110,116)sts.
Work 2½ in (6 cm) k2, p2 rib, ending with a right-side row.
Inc. row: Rib 5(8,3,6), * inc. in next st., rib 14(14,12,12), rep. from * to last 5(8,3,6)sts., inc. in next st., rib to end: 107(113,119,125)sts.

JEAN HARLOW
1911-1937

'The "T" is silent as in Harlot' explained Margot Asquith to Jean Harlow after Harlow insisted on repeatedly mispronouncing Margot's name. The enthusiasm of one of Hollywood's most famous platinum blondes was legendary. Curvaceous, vivacious and bubbly as champagne were three popular descriptions of this extraordinary, nubile creature.

She was born in Kansas City, Missouri, in 1911, and eloped at 16. While working as a film extra in Los Angeles, she was discovered by the famous Howard Hughes when casting for *Hell's Angels* (1930), and shot to stardom.

Her great gifts as a comedienne were first displayed in Capra's *Platinum Blonde* (1931). Soon she was teamed with Clark Gable in *Red Dust* (1932); the chemistry worked and she went on to make several successful films with Gable, including *Hold Your Man* (1933) and *China Seas* (1935).

Some of the most blatantly sexual photographs taken in Hollywood were of Jean Harlow. Refusing to wear underclothes, she poured herself into low-cut slinky, satin gowns which left little to the imagination, but though her image was scandalous in the 1930s, she was always affectionately tarty, a happy-go-lucky good-time gal who almost always got her man. She is probably best remembered in *Dinner at Eight* (1933), a role which allowed Harlow to show off to best advantage her special brand of acting – a combination of comedienne, coquette and everybody's favorite slut.

Sadly, she died of uremic poisoning aged only 26 before she could complete *Saratoga* (1937) with Clark Gable.

Change to size 4 (3¾ mm) needles.
Beg. k row, work in st.st. until back measures 13 in (33 cm), ending with a p row.
Shape armholes
Bind off 3(3,3,4)sts. at beg. of next 2 rows, 2(2,3,3)sts. at beg. of next 2 rows, then 2 sts. at beg. of following 2(6,6,6) rows.
Dec. 1 st. at beg. of next 8(4,4,6) rows: 85(87,91,93)sts.
Work even until back measures 21¼ (21½,22,22½)in/54(55,56,57)cm from beg., ending with a p row.
Shape shoulders and neck
Bind off 5(6,6,6)sts. at beg. of next 2 rows and 6 sts. at beg. of following 2 rows.
Next row: Bind off 6(6,6,7)sts., k16 (16,18,18)sts. (including st. left on needle after binding off), bind off next 19 sts., k to end.
Work on first set of 22(22,24,25)sts.
Next row: Bind off 6(6,6,7)sts., p to end.
Next row: Bind off 10(10,11,11)sts., k to end.
Bind off remaining 6(6,7,7)sts.
Return to remaining sts.
With wrong side facing, rejoin yarn and p to end.
Now complete to match first side of neck, reversing all shaping.

· FRONT ·

Work as given for back until front measures 11½(12,12¼,12½)in/29(30, 31,32)cm, ending with a p row.
Divide for front opening
Next row: K50(53,56,59), bind off 1 st., k to end.
Work on last set of sts. for right front as follows:
1st and 2nd sizes only
Next row: P to end.
Next row: Bind off 2 sts., k to end.
P 1 row, then bind off 1 st. at neck edge on next row, 2 sts. on following alternate row and 1 st. on following alter-

nate row.

Work 2(4) rows even, so ending at armhole edge.

Shape armhole

Bind off 3 sts. at beg. of next row and 2 sts. at beg. of following 2(4) alternate rows.

Dec. 1 st. at armhole edge on following 4(2) alternate rows: 39(40)sts.

3rd size only

Next row: P to end.

Next row: Bind off 2 sts., k to end.

P 1 row, then bind off 1 st. at neck edge on next row and 2 sts. on following alternate row.

Shape armhole

Bind off 3 sts. at beg. of next row and 1 st. at neck edge at beg. of following row.

Keeping neck edge straight, bind off 3 sts. at armhole edge at beg. of next row, then 2 sts. at beg. of following 3 alternate rows and 1 st. at beg. of 2 following alternate rows: 42 sts.

4th size only

Next row: P to end.

Next row: Bind off 2 sts., k to end.

Shape armhole

Bind off 4 sts. at beg. of next row, 1 st. at beg. of next, 3 sts. at beg. of next, then 2 sts. at beg. of following 2 rows.

Bind off 1 st. at neck edge at beg. of next row.

Keeping neck edge straight, bind off 2 sts. at beg. of next and following alternate row, then 1 st. at beg. of following 3 alternate rows: 43 sts.

All sizes

Work even until front measures 19½ (20,20½,21)in / 50(51,52,53)cm from beg., ending at neck edge.

Shape neck

Next row: Bind off 4 sts., work to end.

Work 1 row.

Bind off 3 sts. at beg. of next row.

Work 1 row.

Bind off 2 sts. at beg. of next and following 2(2,3,3) alternate rows, then 1 st. at beg. of following 2(2,1,1) alternate rows, so ending at armhole edge.

Shape shoulder

Bind off 5(6,6,6)sts. at beg. of next row and 1 st. at beg. of following row.

Keeping neck edge straight, bind off 6 sts. at beg. of next row, then 6(6,6,7)sts. at beg. of following alternate row.

Work 1 row, then bind off remaining 6(6,7,7)sts.

Return to remaining sts.

With wrong side facing, rejoin yarn to remaining sts. and p to end.

Work even until front measures 13 in (33 cm) from beg., ending at armhole edge.

Shape armhole

Bind off 3(3,3,4)sts. at beg. of next row, then 2(2,3,3)sts. at beg. of following alternate row.

Bind off 2 sts. at armhole edge on following 1(3,3,3) alternate rows, then bind off 1 st. on following 4(2,2,3) alternate rows: 39(40,42,43)sts.

Now complete to match first side of neck, reversing all shaping.

· SHORT SLEEVES ·

Using size 1 (2¾ mm) needles cast on 72(76,80,84)sts.

Work 1 in (3 cm) k2, p2 rib, ending with a right-side row.

Inc. row: Rib 1(3,5,7), * inc. in next st., rib 9, rep. from * to last 1(3,5,7)sts., inc. in next st., rib to end: 80(84,88,92)sts.

Change to size 4 (3¾) mm needles.

Working in st.st., inc. 1 st. each end of 3rd and every following 4th row until there are 90(94,98,102)sts.

Work even until sleeve measures 4 in (10 cm) from beg., ending with a p row.

Shape top

Bind off 3(3,3,4)sts. at beg. of next 2 rows and 2 sts. at beg. of following 18(22,24,26) rows: 48(44,44,42)sts.

Dec. 1 st. at beg. of next 12(8,8,6) rows.

Bind off 2 sts. at beg. of next 6 rows, then 3 sts. at beg. of following 2 rows.

Bind off remaining 18 sts.

· LONG SLEEVES ·

Using size 1 (2¾ mm) needles cast on 50(54,58,62)sts.

Work 2¼ in (6 cm) k2, p2 rib, ending with a right-side row.

Inc. row: Rib 4(2,1,3), * inc. in next st., rib 5(6,7,7), rep. from * to last 4(3,1,3)sts., inc. in next st., rib to end: 58(62,66,70)sts.

Change to size 4 (3¾ mm) needles.

Working in st.st., inc. 1 st. each end of 7th and every following 8th row to 70(76,82,88)sts., then every following 6th row to 90(94,98,102)sts.

Work even until sleeve measures 42(43,44,45)cm., ending with a p row.

Shape top as given for short sleeve.

· BUTTONHOLE BORDER ·

Using size 1 (2¾ mm) needles cast on 3 sts.

Rib row 1: (Right side) K2, p1.

Rib row 2: Inc. in first st., p1, k1.

Rib row 3: K2, p1, inc. in last st.

Rib row 4: Inc. in first st., [p1, k1] twice.

Rib row 5: K2, p1, k1, p1, inc. in last st.

Keeping rib correct, continue to inc. 1 st. at shaped edge on next 6 rows: 13 sts.

Rib 1 row.

Buttonhole row: Rib 5, bind off 2 sts., rib to end.

Next row: Rib to end, casting on 2 sts. over those bound off in previous row.

Continue in rib, working 4 more buttonholes roughly 1 in (3 cm) apart, then work 4 rows in rib.

Bind off in rib.

· BUTTON BORDER ·

Work to match buttonhole border, omitting the buttonholes.

· COLLAR ·

Using size 2 (3 mm) needles cast on 113(113,117,117)sts.

Rib row 1: K2, * p1, k1, rep. from * to last st., k1.

Rib row 2: K1, * p1, k1, rep. from * to end.

Rep. these 2 rows for 2 in (5 cm).

Change to size 1 (2¾ mm) needles and continue in rib until collar measures 3½ in (9 cm) from beg., ending with a wrong-side row.

Shape neck

Rows 1 and 2: Rib to last 12(12, 13,13)sts., turn.

Rows 3 and 4: Rib to last 12 sts., turn leaving 24(24,25,25)sts. altogether unworked.

Rows 5 and 6: Rib to last 13 sts., turn leaving 37(37,38,38)sts. altogether unworked.

Next row: Rib to end of row, including the unworked sts.

Next row: Rib across all 113 (113, 117,117)sts.

Bind off in rib.

· FINISHING ·

Join shoulder seams. Sew in sleeves, then join side and sleeve seams. Sew on front borders, overlapping right over left and neatly stitching shaped edges at center front. Sew bind-off edge of collar to neck edge, placing side edges of collar to center of front borders. Sew on buttons.

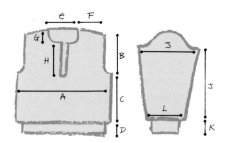

A	19	(20,	21¼,	22½)	in
	48	(51,	54,	57)	cm
B	8¼	(8¾,	9,	9½)	in
	21	(22,	23,	24)	cm
C	10¾				in
	27				cm
D	2¼				in
	6				cm
E	7	(7,	7½,	7½)	in
	18	(18,	19,	19)	cm
F	3¾	(4,	4¼,	4½)	in
	10	(10.5,	11,	11.5)	cm
G	2¼				in
	6				cm
H	8¼				in
	21				cm

I	16	(17,	17¾,	18)	in
	41	(43,	45,	46)	cm
J	16½	(17,	17½,	17¾)	in
	42	(43,	44,	45)	cm
K	2¼				in
	6				cm
L	10¼	(11,	11¾,	12½)	in
	26	(28,	30,	32)	cm
M	16	(17,	17¾,	18)	in
	41	(43,	45,	46)	cm
N	2¾				in
	7				cm
O	1¼				in
	3				cm
P	14	(15,	15¾,	16½)	in
	36	(38,	40,	42)	cm

A sexy, bare-midriff top knitted in fluffy angora which will show off your tan even on cooler days. The short top with slightly gathered, set-in sleeves and round neck is quick to knit in basic stockinette stitch, but the effect is glamorous.

· MEASUREMENTS ·

To fit bust 32(34,36,38)in/81(86,91, 97)cm
Actual measurements 32(34,36,38)in/ 81(86,91,97)cm
Length to shoulders 13½(13½,14½, 14½)in/34(34,37,37)cm
Sleeve seam 3 in (8 cm)

· MATERIALS ·

13(14,15,16) × 10g balls Georges Picaud 100% Angora
A pair each of size 5 (4 mm) and size 6 (4½ mm) knitting needles

· GAUGE ·

20 sts. and 30 rows to 4 in (10 cm) over st.st. using size 6 (4½ mm) needles.

· BACK ·

* Using size 5 (4 mm) needles cast on 69(73,79,83)sts.
Rib row 1: K1, * p1, k1, rep. from * to end.
Rib row 2: P1, * k1, p1, rep. from * to end.
Rep. these 2 rows for 1 in (3 cm), ending with rib row 1.
Inc. row: Rib 6(8,4,6), * M1, rib 4(4,5,5), rep. from * to last 7(9,5,7)sts., M1, rib to end: 84(88,94,98)sts.
Change to size 6 (4½ mm) needles.
Proceed in st.st. until back measures 6(6,6½,6½)in/15(15,17,17)cm from beg., ending with a p row.

ADELE JERGENS

1922 ☞

Adele Jergens is not, as her name suggests, yet another mid European import. She was actually born in Brooklyn New York in 1922. 5′6½″ tall, this brassy, pert, platinum blonde was nevertheless something of a celebrity in her youth, gaining publicity as the undoubted winner of the 'Miss World's Fairest' contest at New York's World Fair in 1939. She was much in demand after this event and decorated many a Broadway show.

Jergens became one of New York's most famous models and a top class showgirl. She entertained in nightclubs in Rio de Janeiro, Biarritz and London amongst many other famous cities. It was on one of these tours that she was spotted by a Columbia Pictures talent scout which led to her first film part in *Tonight and Every Night* (1945). In *Edge of Doom* (1950) she played opposite Dana Andrews and Farley Granger. It was a fine performance as the dame who always gets the blame – and the bullet.

Although she sometimes played the lead she more often played the second lead in generally low budget movies, forever cast as the brazen blonde or the archetypal gangster's moll. It is doubtful whether she enjoyed being typecast in this way but she nevertheless always attacked her roles with enthusiastic gusto.

Posing was as natural to her as breathing; her modeling days had trained her well to command the camera. She looked best in the bare essentials – a snappy pair of shorts, a midriff sweater and a happy-go-lucky smile – but she could also train an evening gown to flow at her will.

Shape armholes
Bind off 6 sts. at beg. of next 2 rows.
Dec. 1 st. each end of every row until 60(60,64,64)sts. remain. *
Work even until armholes measure 7½(7½,8,8)in/19(19,20,20)cm from beg., ending with a p row.
Shape shoulders
Bind off 9(9,10,10)sts. at beg. of next 4 rows.
Break off yarn and leave remaining 24 sts. on a holder.

· FRONT ·

Work as given for back from * to *.
Work even until armholes measure 5(5,5½,5½)in/13(13,14,14)cm from beg., ending with a p row.
Shape neck
Next row: K24(24,26,26), turn and leave remaining sts. on a spare needle.
Work 1 row.
Dec. 1 st. at neck edge on next and every following alternate row until 18(18,20,20)sts. remain.
Work even until front measures same as back to shoulders, ending at armhole edge.
Shape shoulder
Bind off 9(9,10,10)sts. at beg. of next row.
Work 1 row. Bind off.
Return to remaining sts.
With right side facing, slip first 12 sts. onto a holder, join on yarn and work second side of neck to match first, reversing all shaping.

· SLEEVES ·

Using size 5 (4 mm) needles cast on 49(49,53,53)sts.
Work the 2 rib rows for 1 in (3 cm), ending with rib row 1.
Inc. row: Rib 2(2,4,4), * M1, rib 3, rep. from * to last 2(2,4,4)sts., M1, rib to end: 65(65,69,69)sts.

ADELE JERGENS
1922 ☞

Change to size 6 (4½ mm) needles.
Proceed in st.st. until work measures
3 in (8 cm) from beg., ending with a
p row.

Shape top

Bind off 6 sts. at beg. of next 2 rows.
Dec. 1 st. at beg. of every row until
49(49,51,51)sts. remain.
Work even until sleeve measures 10¼
(10¼,10½,10½)in / 26(26,27,27)cm
from beg., ending with a p row.
Bind off 5 sts. at beg. of next 8 rows.
Bind off remaining 9(9,11,11)sts.

· NECKBAND ·

Join right shoulder seam.
With right side facing and using size 5
(4 mm) needles, pick up and k20 sts.
down left side of front neck, k across 12
sts. from front neck holder, pick up
and k21 sts. up right side of front neck,
then k across 24 sts. from back neck
holder: 77 sts.
Beg. rib row 2, work 5 rows in rib.
Bind off in rib.

· FINISHING ·

Join left shoulder and neckband seam.
Sew in sleeves, gathering at top to fit.
Join side and sleeve seams.

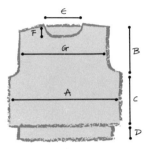

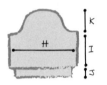

A	16½	(17½,	18½,	19)	in
	42	(44,	47,	48)	cm
B	7½	(7½,	7¾,	7¾)	in
	19	(19,	20,	20)	cm
C	4¾	(4¾,	5½,	5½)	in
	12	(12,	14,	14)	cm
D	1¼				in
	3				cm
E	4¾				in
	12				cm
F	2¼				in
	6				cm
G	12	(12,	12½,	12½)	in
	30	(30,	32,	32)	cm
H	12¾	(12¾,	13½,	13½)	in
	32.5	(32.5,	34.5,	34.5)	cm
I	2				in
	5				cm
J	1¼				in
	3				cm
K	8¼	(8¼,	8¾,	8¾)	in
	21	(21,	22,	22)	cm

This longline sweater is knitted in half fisherman's rib with deep turned back cuffs and collar, and a button front opening. This version has updated raglan sleeves and saddle shoulders, ideal for wearing over layers. Made in a chunky yarn on big needles, it knits up quicker than you'd think.

· MEASUREMENTS ·

To fit bust 30–32(34–36,38–40)in/ 76–81(86–92, 97–102)cm
Actual measurements 46(49,53¾)in/ 116(124,136)cm
Length to shoulders:
Sweater: 24(26¼,28¾)in/61(67,73)cm
Dress: 37¾(40,42½)in/96(102,108)cm
Sleeve seam 16 in (41 cm)

· MATERIALS ·

Sweater: 30(32,32) × 50g balls Scheepjeswol Superwash Plus
Dress: 38(40,42) × 50g balls Scheepjeswol Superwash Plus
A pair each of size 9 (6 mm) and size 12 (8 mm) knitting needles
Size J (6.00 mm) crochet hook; 6 buttons

· GAUGE ·

10½ sts. and 20 rows to 4 in (10 cm) over pattern using size 12 (8 mm) needles and using yarn double.

· NOTE ·

The yarn for this design is used double throughout. The weight of the wool may cause the garment to stretch and length measurements are slightly shorter to compensate.

JENNIFER JONES

1919-☞

Phyllis Isley was born in Tulsa, Oklahoma in 1919. She emerged as Jennifer Jones after David O. Selznick renamed her in 1939. She had made a couple of unremarkable films before she met Selznick (who became her second husband in 1949). It was largely due to him that her film career matured and strengthened as it did. This brown-haired, brown-eyed beauty scored an early success as the peasant girl from Lourdes who saw visions of the Virgin Mary in *The Song of Bernadette* (1943). Although she was reputed to be camera shy and nervous of performing in front of a studio team she turned in a powerful performance which earned her an Academy Award as Best Actress.

An obsessed Selznick continued to mould her image, wanting only the best roles for his protégée. The most memorable was *Duel in the Sun* (1946) in which, displaying her versatility, she played a wily temptress – a far cry from Bernadette. A number of rather unremarkable films followed, until in 1955 she starred in *Love is a Many-Splendored Thing*, and in 1957 came *A Farewell to Arms*.

Jennifer Jones was a strange enigmatic creature, full of hidden depths. Her role as a near-oriental in *Love is a Many-Splendored Thing* started a trend towards Far Eastern fashions, and magazines of the time were full of the distinctive high-necked, cap-sleeved cut. She aged gracefully and in the 1960s and 1970s played sympathetic, mature women, most notably in *The Towering Inferno* in 1974.

· FRONT ·

Using size 9 (6 mm) needles and yarn double, cast on 55(61,65)sts.
Rib row 1: P1, * k1, p1, rep. from * to end.
Rib row 2: K1, * p1, k1, rep. from * to end.
Rep. these 2 rows for 2¼ in (6 cm), ending with rib row 2.
Change to size 12 (8 mm) needles.
Proceed in patt. as follows:
Row 1: (Right side) K to end.
Row 2: K1, p1, * K1B, p1, rep. from * to last st., k1.
These 2 rows form the patt.
Continue in patt., increasing 1 st. each end of the 11th and every following 12th row until there are 61(67,71)sts.
Work even until front measures 12¼ (13½,14½)in/31(34,37)cm from beg., ending with a wrong-side row.
For dress only
Work a further 13¾in (35 cm) straight in pattern.
Divide for front opening for sweater and dress.
Next row: Patt. 28(31,33), turn and leave remaining sts. on a spare needle.
* Continue on these sts. only until work measures 3½ in (9 cm) from division, ending at armhole edge.
Shape armhole
Bind off 2(2,3)sts. at beg. of next row.
Dec. 1 st. at armhole edge on next and every following 8th(6th,6th) row until 21(22,22)sts. remain, then dec. 1 st. at same edge on following 1(2,2) alternate rows: 20 sts.
Work 1 row. *
Shape neck
Next row: Patt. to last 2 sts., work 2 tog.
Next 2 rows: K to last 3 sts., turn and patt. to last 2 sts., work 2 tog.
Next 2 rows: K to last 6 sts., turn and patt. to end.
Next row: Bind off in patt. 12 sts., break off yarn and leave remaining sts. on a holder.

JENNIFER JONES
1919 ☞

Return to remaining sts.

With right side facing, join on yarn and bind off first 5 sts., patt. to end.

Work as given for first side of neck from * to *.

Next row: K to last 2 sts., work 2 tog.

Next 2 rows: Patt. to last 3 sts., turn and k to last 2 sts., work 2 tog.

Next 2 rows: Patt. to last 6 sts., turn and k to end.

Next row: Bind off in patt. 12 sts., break off yarn and leave remaining sts. on a holder.

· B A C K ·

Omitting front opening work as given for front until back measures the same as front to armholes, ending with a wrong-side row.

Shape armholes

Bind off 2(2,3)sts. at beg. of next 2 rows.

Dec. 1 st. each end of next and every following 6th row until 47(49,49)sts. remain, then each end of every row until 33 sts. remain, so ending with a wrong-side row.

Bind off 8 sts:, patt. to last 8 sts., bind off these 8 sts.

Break off yarn and leave remaining 17 sts. on a holder.

· S L E E V E S ·

Using size 9 (6 mm) needles and an oddment of contrasting yarn cast on 21 sts. and work tubular edge as follows:

Foundation row: Using main yarn double, K1, * yf., k1, rep. from * to end: 41 sts.

Change to size 12 (8 mm) needles.

Row 1: With ytf, sl1, * ytb., k1, ytf., sl1, rep. from * to end.

Row 2: K1, * ytf., sl1, ytb., k1, rep. from * to end.

Rep. these 2 rows once more.

Now continue to work in rib patt. as given for front until sleeve measures 4

in (10 cm) from beg., ending with a right-side row.

Change to size 9 (6 mm) needles.

Patt. 3 rows.

Next row: P1, * k1B, p1, rep. from * to end.

Next row: K to end.

Rep. the last 2 rows twice more.

Change to size 12 (8 mm) needles and continue in patt., increasing and working into rib patt. 1 st. each end of next and every following 4th row until there are 55(61,67)sts.

Work even until sleeve measures 16 in (41 cm) from cast-on edge, ending with a wrong-side row.

Shape top

Bind off 2 sts. at beg. of next 2 rows.

Dec. 1 st. each end of next and every following alternate row until 11 sts. remain, so ending with a right-side row.

Mark end of last row with a colored thread for left sleeve and at beg. of last row for right sleeve.

Keeping marked edge straight, continue decreasing at other edge until 7 sts. remain.

Work even until straight edge is long enough, when slightly stretched, to fit along shoulder section of front.

Break off yarn and leave remaining sts. on a holder.

· B U T T O N H O L E B A N D ·

With right side facing and using size 9 (6 mm) needles, pick up and k47 sts. up right side of front opening.

Beg. rib row 1, work 5 rows rib as given for front.

Buttonhole row 1: Rib 4, [bind off next st., rib 9] 4 times, bind off next st., rib to end.

Buttonhole row 2: Rib to end, casting on 1 st. over those cast off in previous row.

Work 4 more rows in rib.

Bind off in rib.

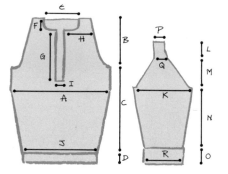

A	23	(25,	27)	in
	58	(64,	68)	cm
B	8¼	(9½,	10¾)	in
	21	(24,	27)	cm
C	13½	(14½,	15½)	in for sweater
	34	(37,	40)	cm for sweater
	27	(28½,	29½)	in for dress
	69	(72,	75)	cm for dress
D	2¼			in
	6			cm
E	6¼			in
	16			cm
F	1¼			in
	3			cm
G	9	(12,	13)	in
	23	(30,	33)	cm
H	7½			in
	19			cm
I	1½			in
	3.5			cm
J	20½	(23,	24½)	in
	52	(58,	62)	cm
K	20½	(23,	25)	in
	52	(58,	64)	cm
L	3¼			in
	8			cm
M	8¼	(9½,	10¾)	in
	21	(24,	27)	cm
N	12¼			in
	31			cm
O	4			in
	10			cm
P	2½			in
	6.5			cm
Q	4¼			in
	10.5			cm
R	15½			in
	39			cm

· BUTTON BAND ·

With right side facing, pick up and k47 sts. down left side of neck opening.
Work 9 rows in rib.
Bind off in rib.

· COLLAR ·

With right side facing and using size 9 (6 mm) needles, pick up and k4 sts. across top of buttonhole band, patt. 6 sts. up right side of neck, 7 sts. across right sleeve top, 17 sts. along back neck, 7 sts. along left sleeve top, 6 sts. down left side of neck, then pick up and k4 sts. along button band: 51 sts.
K 1 row.

Shape collar

Next 2 rows: Patt. to last 20 sts., turn and k to last 20 sts., turn.

Next 2 rows: Patt. to last 18 sts., turn and k to last 18 sts., turn.

Next 2 rows: Patt. to last 16 sts., turn and k to last 16 sts., turn.

Continue in this way, working 2 more sts. before turning on every 2 rows until all the sts. of collar are being worked.

Continue in patt. over all sts. until front edge of collar measures size 18 in (46 cm), ending at buttonhole band edge.

Next 2 rows: K to last st., turn and patt. to last st., turn.

Next 2 rows: K to last 3 sts., turn and patt., to last 3 sts., turn.

Next 2 rows: K to last 5 sts., turn and patt. to last 5 sts., turn.

Continue in this way, working 2 sts. less each end until 2 rows have been worked as follows: k to last 19 sts., turn and patt. to last 19 sts., turn.

Next row: K to end, so ending at button band edge.

Work 1 more row over all sts.
Bind off loosely in patt.

· FINISHING ·

Join raglan seams, fitting side edges of sleeve top to bind-off sts. along shoulder sections of back and front.

Turn collar in half to wrong side and slipstitch into position.

Join side and sleeve seams, reversing cuff seams for last 4 in (10 cm).

Stitch lower edges of front bands to bind-off sts. at center front.

Work a row of single crochet along front edges of collar, working through both thicknesses.

Make a button loop on right front edge of collar approximately 2¾ in (7 cm) up from buttonhole band.

Sew on buttons to correspond with buttonholes, and one button onto underside of collar, approximately 2¾ in (7 cm) up from button band and 1 in (3 cm) in from the edge, to correspond with button loop.

This slim-fitting boat-necked top is worked throughout in basic stockinette stitch. The top has short raglan sleeves with double ribbed bands. If you have one, you may find a circular needle useful for working the wide neckband. The beads can be sewn on afterwards to add glamor.

· MEASUREMENTS ·

To fit bust 32(34,36,38)in/81(86,91, 97)cm

Actual measurements 36¼(38,40¼, 42)in/92(96,102,106)cm

Length to shoulders 18(18,19,19¼) in/45.5(46,48.5,49)cm

Sleeve seam 2¾ in (7 cm)

· MATERIALS ·

4(5,6,7) × 50g ball Robin Sundance D.K.

A pair each of size 3 (3¼ mm) and size 5 (4 mm) knitting needles

· GAUGE ·

24 sts. and 32 rows to 4 in (10 cm) over st.st. using size 5 (4 mm) needles.

· BACK AND FRONT ·
(Alike)

Using size 3 (3¼ mm) needles cast on 110(116,122,128)sts.

Work 2 in (5 cm) k2, p2 rib.

Change to size 5 (4 mm) needles.

Beg. k row, proceed in st.st. until work measures 11¼(11¼,12,12)in/29(29, 31,31)cm from beg., ending with a p row.

Shape raglans

Bind off 6 sts. at beg. of next 2 rows.

Dec. 1 st. each end of next and every

DOROTHY LAMOUR
1914 ☞

In a studio portrait taken in 1936 by Ernest A. Bachrach, Dorothy Lamour's features, although she was brunette, are not dissimilar to those of today's pop star Madonna. Indeed, Lamour started her career as a singer in Chicago. Her slightly exotic looks led to her first movie *The Jungle Princess* (1936), and she was to spend most of her film career in exotic settings draped in a sarong. Although she begged the studio to consider her for more substantial roles Miss Lamour and the sarong were big at the box office. When the U.S. marines were engaged in warfare in the South Pacific, Dorothy epitomized their ideal South Sea Island Beauty.

Her most memorable films were the *Road* series: *Road to Singapore* (1940), *Zanzibar* (1941), *Morocco* (1942), *Utopia* (1945), *Rio* (1947) and *Bali* (1952). Teamed with the dynamic duo, Bing Crosby and Bob Hope, these successful movies made her a household name, which was good news for the ex-Miss New Orleans (1931), where she was born. The chemistry between Lamour and Hope brought out a special ingredient in her that transcended the ordinary.

She had a voluptuous figure, tending towards plumpness. She carried herself well and always looked good, and had the enviable ability to make a potato sack look like a couture garment. She was a great success in one of the touring versions of *Hello Dolly* in the 1960s and has appeared frequently on TV, but she refuses to make another movie until she is offered more interesting material – with no sarong.

following 4th row to 80(86,92,98)sts., then dec. 1 st. each end of next and every following alternate row until 72(76,80,84)sts. remain.

Shape neck

Next row: K2 tog., k20, turn and leave remaining sts. on a spare needle. Continuing to dec. at raglan edge on every alternate row as before, bind off 4 sts. at neck edge at beg. of next and following 3 alternate rows.

K2 tog. and fasten off.

Return to remaining sts.

With right side facing, slip first 28(32,36,40)sts. onto a holder, rejoin yarn and k to last 2 sts., k2 tog.

Work 1 row, then complete to match first side of neck, reversing all shaping.

· SLEEVES ·

Using size 3 (3¼ mm) needles cast on 70(72,74,76)sts.

Work 1 in (2.5 cm) k1, p1 rib.

Change to size 5 (4 mm) needles.

Beg. with a k row, work in st.st. increasing 1 st. each end of first and every following 4th row until there are 78(80,82,84)sts., ending with a p row.

Shape raglan

Bind off 6 sts. at beg. of next 2 rows.

Dec. 1 st. each end of next and every following 4th row to 48(50,52,54)sts., then dec. 1 st. each end of every following alternate row until 32 sts. remain, ending with a p row.

Break off yarn and leave sts. on a holder.

· NECKBAND ·

Join raglan seams, leaving left back raglan open.

With right side facing and using size 3 (3¼ mm) needles, k32 sts. from left sleeve holder, pick up and k16 sts. down left side of front neck, k28(32, 36,40)sts. from center front holder,

DOROTHY LAMOUR
1914 ☞

pick up and k16 sts. up right side of front neck, k32 sts. from right sleeve holder, pick up and k16 sts. down right side of back neck, k28(32,36,40)sts. from back neck holder, then pick up and k16 sts. up left side of back neck: 184(192,200,208)sts.
Work 7 rows k1, p1 rib.
Bind off in rib.

· FINISHING ·

Join left back raglan and neckband seam.
Join side and sleeve seams.

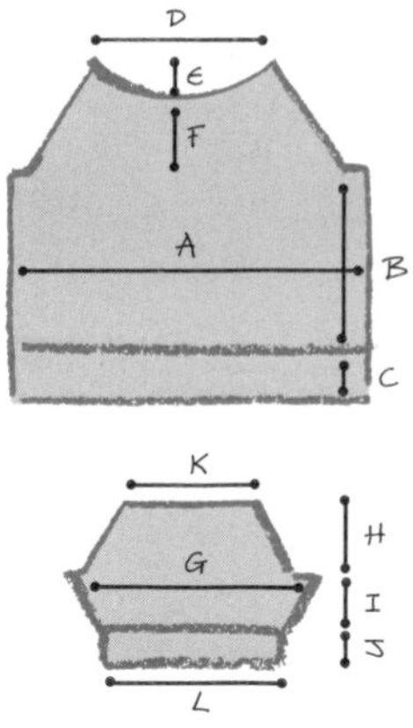

A	*18* 46	*(19,* (48,	*20,* 51,	*21)* 53)	*in* cm
B	*9½* 24	*(9½,* (24,	*10¼,* 26,	*10¼)* 26)	*in* cm
C	*2* 5	*in* cm			
D	*9¾* 25	*(10¾,* (27,	*11,* 28,	*12)* 30)	*in* cm
E	*1* 2.5	*in* cm			
F	*5½* 14	*(5¾,* (14.5,	*6,* 15,	*6¼)* 15.5)	*in* cm
G	*12¾* 32.5	*(13,* (33,	*13½,* 34,	*13¾)* 35)	*in* cm
H	*6¼* 15.5	*(6½,* (16,	*6¾,* 17,	*7)* 17.5)	*in* cm
I	*1¾* 4.5	*in* cm			
J	*1* 2.5	*in* cm			
K	*5¼* 13	*in* cm			
L	*11½* 29	*(12,* (30,	*12¼,* 31,	*12¾)* 32)	*in* cm

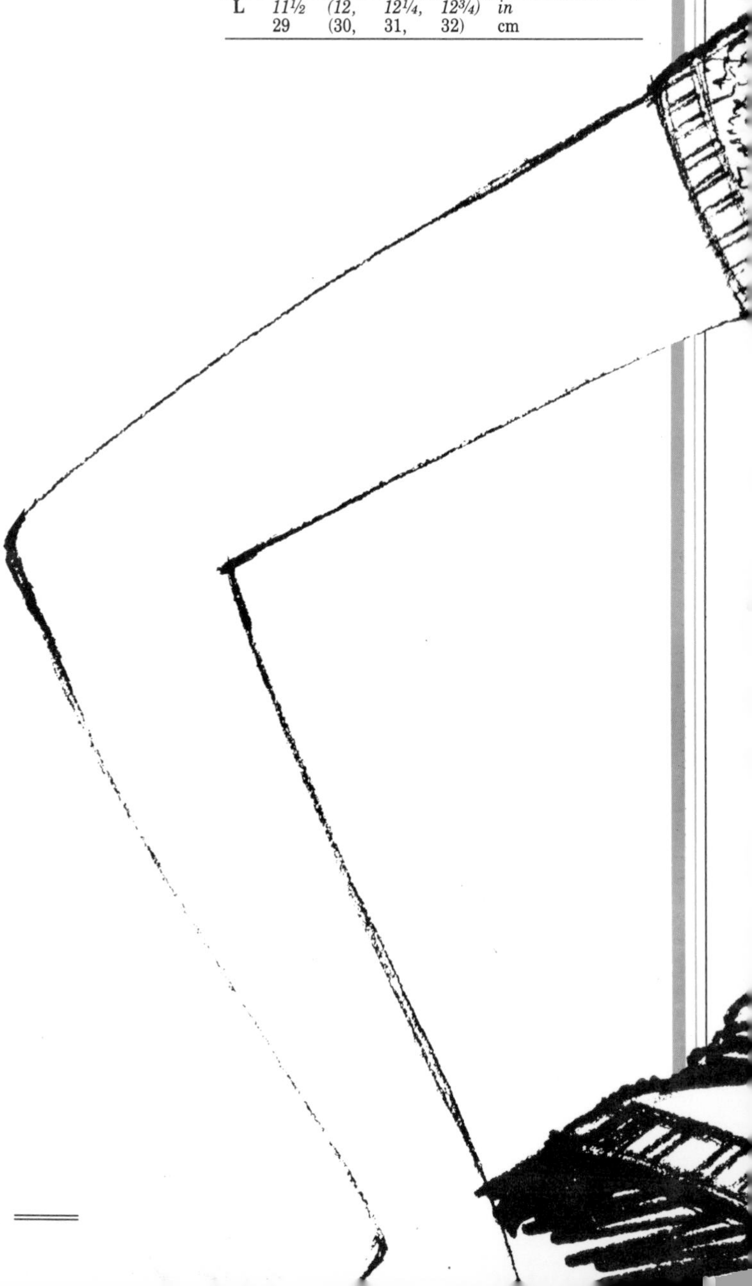

This picture sweater in simple stockinette stitch is not strictly for the birds! The bird design is repeated on the back, with the set-in sleeves left plain. The ribbing and decorative armhole borders are in double rib with the neckband slipstitched inside to give a neat finish.

· MEASUREMENTS ·

To fit bust 32(34,36,38)in/81(86,91,97)cm
Actual measurements 36(38,39½,41½)in/91(96,101,106)cm
Length to shoulders 21¼(21½,21½,21½)in/54(54.5,55,55.5)cm
Sleeve seam 16½(16½,17,17)in/42(42,43,43)cm

· MATERIALS ·

8(9,9,10) × 50g balls Silk City Chandos in main color A
1 ball each of same in contrast colors B, C and D
A pair each of size 3 (3¼ mm) and size 5 (4 mm) knitting needles

· GAUGE ·

22 sts. and 30 rows to 4 in (10 cm) over st.st. using size 5 (4 mm) needles.

· FRONT ·

* With size 3 (3¼ mm) needles and A, cast on 78(86,90,98)sts.
Rib row 1: K2, * p2, k2, rep. from * to end.
Rib row 2: P2, * k2, p2, rep. from * to end.
Rep. these 2 rows for 3 in (8 cm), ending with rib row 1.
Inc. row: Rib 6(7,7,8), * M1, rib 6(8,7,9), rep. from * to last 6(7,6,9)sts., M1, rib 6(7,6,9): 90(96,102,108)sts. *

VIRGINIA MAYO

1920 ☞

Costume dramas of the 1950s were not renowned for their historical accuracy, and *King Richard and the Crusades* (1954) was a typical example. Virginia Mayo played a very 1950s Queen Berengaria to George Sanders' Richard the Lionheart, but to audiences of the day Mayo's appearance was almost enough to carry any film. Indeed, Virginia Jones, as she was born, was once described by the Sultan of Morocco as 'tangible proof of the existence of God' – a flattering comment for the hazel-eyed, ash-blonde beauty from St Louis.

She started her career as a ballet dancer, moved from ballet to Vaudeville, and eventually to the Sam Goldwyn stable where she was put through the famous Hollywood process of glamorization. On film, Virginia Mayo is rarely seen facially full frontal; she was always shot at every other conceivable angle because of a slight eye defect.

Mayo starred in light-hearted, frothy escapist movies that demanded her to look glamorous and alluring but also slightly quizzical. The most memorable of this genre was *The Secret Life of Walter Mitty* (1947) in which she starred opposite Danny Kaye. She had some straight dramatic parts, notably in *The Best Years of Our Lives* (1946) but will forever be associated with films which portrayed her as a voluptuous and stunning blonde, immaculately dressed. She was one of World War II's favorite pin-ups and the kind of 'gal' who could take men's minds off the cares and woes of everyday existence into a world of make-believe and enticing fantasy.

Change to size 5 (4 mm) needles.
Use separate small balls of yarn for each area of color and twist yarns together on WS of work when changing color to avoid making a hole.
Reading odd numbered (k) rows from right to left and even numbered (p) rows from left to right, work in patt. from chart increasing 1 st. each end of every 10th row until there are 100 (106,112,118)sts.
Continue in patt. from chart until row 80 has been completed.
Shape armholes
Bind off 6(7,8,9)sts. at beg. of next 2 rows.
Keeping patt. correct, dec. 1 st. each end of every following row until 76(80,84,88)sts. remain, then every following alternate row to 72(76,80,84)sts.
Work even until row 113 of chart has been completed.
Working in A only, continue in st.st. for a further 7(7,11,11) rows.
Shape neck
Next row: K27(29,31,33)sts., turn and leave remaining sts. on a spare needle.
Work on first set of sts. as follows:
Dec. 1 st. at neck edge on next 4 rows, then on every following alternate row until 19(20,21,22)sts. remain.
Work 5(5,1,1) rows even, so ending at armhole edge.
Shape shoulders
Bind off 10 sts. at beg. of next row.
Work 1 row, then bind off.
Return to remaining sts.
With right side facing, slip first 18 sts. onto a holder, k to end.
Now complete to match first side of neck, reversing all shaping.

· BACK ·

Work as given for front from * to *.
Change to size 5 (4 mm) needles.
Working in A only, inc. 1 st. each end

VIRGINIA MAYO
1920

of every 10th row until there are 100(106,112,118)sts.
Work even until 80 rows st.st. have been worked.

Shape armholes

Bind off 6(7,8,9)sts. at beg. of next 2 rows.
Dec. 1 st. each end of every row until 76(80,84,88)sts. remain, then on every following alternate row until 72(76, 80,84)sts. remain, ending with p row.
Work 10 rows even, ending with p row.
Beg. at row 92 of chart for back, work bird motifs, omitting leaves as follows:
Next row: P9(11,13,15)A, 15B, 24A, 15B, 9(11,13,15)A.
Next row: K13(15,17,19)A, 1C, 3A, 1C, 36A, 1C, 3A, 1C, 13(15,17,19)A.
Continue from chart in this way, omitting the center leaf motifs, until row 113 has been completed.
Work even until back measures same as back to shoulders, ending with a p row.

Shape shoulders

Bind off 10 sts. at beg. of next 2 rows and 9(10,11,12)sts. at beg. of following 2 rows.
Break off yarn and leave remaining 34(36,38,40)sts. on a holder.

· SLEEVES ·

Using size 3 (3¼ mm) needles and A, cast on 44(48,52,56)sts.
Work in k2, p2 rib for 3 in (8 cm), ending with a right-side row.
Inc. row: Rib 2(6,1,4), * M1, rib 4(4, 5,5), rep. from * to last 2(2,1,2)sts., rib 2(2,1,2): 54(58,62,66)sts.
Change to size 5 (4 mm) needles.
Working in st.st., inc. 1 st. each end of 5th and every following 6th row until there are 84(88,92,96)sts.
Work even until sleeve measures 16½ (16½,17,17)in/42(42,43,43)cm, ending with a p row.

Shape top

Bind off 6(7,8,9)sts. at beg. of next 2 rows.
Dec. 1 st. each end of next 6 rows, then 1 st. each end of every following alternate row until 38 sts. remain.
Dec. 1 st. each end of every row until 22 sts. remain.
Bind off 4 sts. at beg. of next 2 rows, then bind off remaining 14 sts.

· NECKBAND ·

Join right shoulder seam.
With right side facing and using size 3 (3¼ mm) needles and A, pick up and k18(19,20,21)sts. down left front neck, k across 18 sts. from front neck holder, pick up and k 18(19,20,21)sts. up right side of front neck, then k across 34(36,38,40)sts. from back neck holder: 88(92,96,100)sts.
Beg. rib row 2, work 2½ in (6 cm) in rib as given for back.
Bind off in rib.

· ARMHOLE BORDERS ·

Using size 3 (3¼ mm) needles and A, cast on 128(132,136,140)sts.
Work 4 rows k2, p2 rib.
Bind off 8 sts. at beg. of next 6 rows.
Bind off in rib.

· FINISHING ·

Join left shoulder and neckband seam. Fold neckband in half to wrong side and slipstitch into place. Tack cast off edges of armhole borders round armhole, then sew in sleeves stitching through all three thicknesses. Join side and sleeve seams. Press lightly following instructions on ball band.

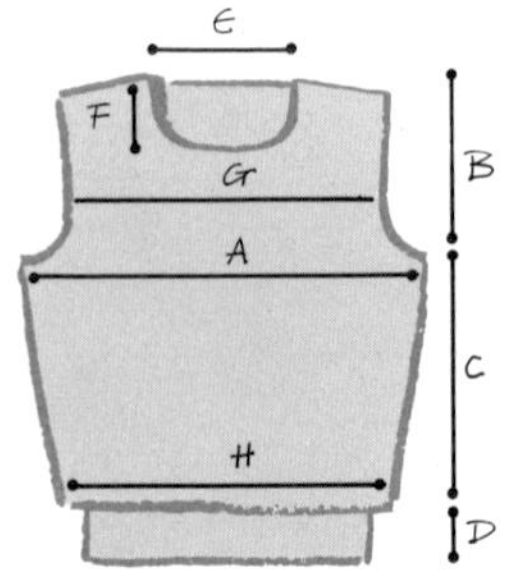

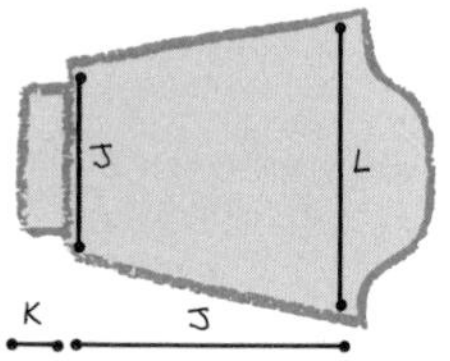

A	*18*	*(19,*	*19¾,*	*21)*	*in*
	45.5	(48,	50.5,	53)	cm
B	*7½*	*(7¾,*	*8,*	*8¼)*	*in*
	19.5	(20,	20.5,	21)	cm
C	*10½*	*in*			
	26.5	cm			
D	*3¼*	*in*			
	8	cm			
E	*5¾*	*(6¼,*	*6¾,*	*7¼)*	*in*
	15	(16,	17,	18)	cm
F	*2¼*	*in*			
	6	cm			
G	*13*	*(13½,*	*14¼,*	*15)*	*in*
	33	(34.5,	36,	38)	cm
H	*16*	*(17½,*	*18,*	*19¼)*	*in*
	41	(44,	46,	49)	cm
I	*15*	*(15¾,*	*16½,*	*17½)*	*in*
	38	(40,	42,	44)	cm
J	*13½*	*(13½,*	*13¾,*	*13¾)*	*in*
	34	(34,	35,	35)	cm
K	*3¼*	*in*			
	8	cm			
L	*9½*	*(10¼,*	*11,*	*12)*	*in*
	24	(26,	28,	30)	cm

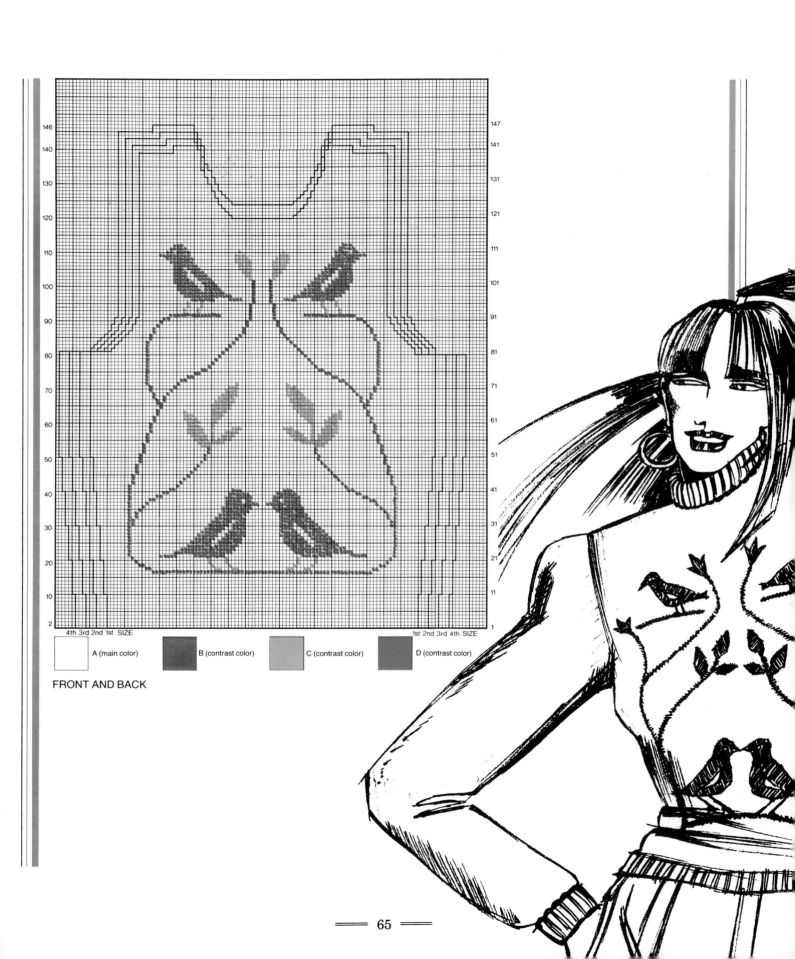

146   147
140   141
130   131
120   121
110   111
100   101
90   91
80   81
70   71
60   61
50   51
40   41
30   31
20   21
10   11
2   1

4th 3rd 2nd 1st SIZE   1st 2nd 3rd 4th SIZE

A (main color)   B (contrast color)   C (contrast color)   D (contrast color)

FRONT AND BACK

This quick-knit sleeveless top looks great layered or worn on its own. It's worked throughout in stockinette stitch and the minimum shaping makes it a good choice for beginners. The round neckline has an unusual, deep single-rib neckband, pinned down asymmetrically with a brooch to great effect by Miss Monroe.

· MEASUREMENTS ·

To fit bust 32(34,36,38)in/81(86,91, 97)cm
Actual measurements 34(35½,37½, 39)in/86(90,95,99)cm
Length to shoulders 20(20½,21,21¼) in/51(52,53,54)cm

· MATERIALS ·

4(4,5,5) × 50g balls Pingouin Confort
A pair each of size 3 (3¼ mm) and size 5 (4 mm) knitting needles

· GAUGE ·

21 sts. and 28 rows to 4 in (10 cm) over st.st. using size 5 (4 mm) needles.

· BACK ·

Using size 3 (3¼ mm) needles cast on 76(80,86,90)sts.
Work 2¾ in (7 cm) k1, p1 rib.
Change to size 5 (4 mm) needles.
Beg. with a k row and working in st.st., dec. 1 st. each end of first and every following 3rd row until 66(70, 76,80)sts. remain.
Work 3 rows even, so ending with a p row.
Now inc. 1 st. each end of next and every following 4th row until there are 90(94,100,104)sts.
Work even until back measures 12½(13,13,13¼)in/32(32.5,33,33.5)cm from beg., ending with a p row.

MARILYN MONROE
1926-1962

Norma Jean Baker was born in Los Angeles, the illegitimate child of a mother who spent most of her life in mental institutions. She wanted to be a star from an early age but studio chiefs were not at first enamoured of her. An early part with Adele Jergens in a B movie *Ladies of the Chorus* (1948) was unremarkable, but two years later she made the skeptics sit up and take notice with her role in John Huston's *The Asphalt Jungle* (1950). From then she was on her way. In 1953 she made *Gentlemen Prefer Blondes* with Jane Russell, and shone as a dizzy gold digger. Her distinct talents as a comedienne were shown to full advantage in *How to Marry a Millionaire* (1953) and *The Seven Year Itch* (1955).

However, like Garland, she was now popping pills to keep going and was becoming increasingly difficult on and off the set. In 1959 she made her most successful film, *Some Like It Hot* with Jack Lemmon and Tony Curtis, but she was only to make two more movies. Increasingly worried by debt, her inability to have children and a fear of aging, this most luminous of stars was found dead from an overdose in 1962. The movie industry has not seen her like again.

Marilyn Monroe spelled sex whatever she wore, from earthy hessian to regal duchess satin. A knitted sweater on Monroe became sensual, diamonds took on a new lustre. There was no amount of folds or drapery that could hide the shapely, sinuous figure. Marilyn Monroe has become a legend among Hollywood filmstars.

Shape armholes

Bind off 2(3,3,4)sts. at beg. of next 2 rows.
Dec. 1 st. each end of next 2 rows, then each end of every following alternate row until 76(78,82,84)sts. remain.
Work even until back measures 20 (20½,21,21¼)in/51(52,53,54)cm from beg., ending with a p row.

Shape shoulders

Bind off 11(11,12,12)sts. at beg. of next 2 rows, then 12(12,13,13)sts. at beg. of following 2 rows.
Break off yarn and leave remaining 30(32,32,34)sts. on a holder.

· FRONT ·

Work as given for back until front measures 16½(17,17,17¼)in/42(43, 43,44)cm from beg., ending with a p row.

Shape neck

Next row: K 34(35,37,38), turn and leave remaining sts. on a spare needle.
Dec. 1 st. at neck edge on every row until 23(23,25,25)sts. remain.
Work even until front measures same as back to shoulder, ending at armhole edge.

Shape shoulder

Bind off 11(11,12,12)sts. at beg. of next row.
Work 1 row, then bind off.
Return to remaining sts.
With right side facing, slip first 8 sts. onto a holder, rejoin yarn and k to end.
Now complete to match first side of neck, reversing all shaping.

· NECKBAND ·

Join right shoulder seam.
With right side facing and using size 3 (3¼ mm) needles, pick up and k21(22,23,24)sts. down left side of front neck, k8 sts. from front neck holder, pick up and k21(22,23, 24)sts. up right side of front neck, then

MARILYN
MONROE
1926-1962

k30(32,32,34)sts. from back neck holder: 80(84,86,90)sts.
Work 3 in (8 cm) k1, p1 rib.
Bind off loosely in rib.

· ARMHOLE EDGINGS ·

Join left shoulder and neckband seam. With right side facing and using size 3 (3¼ mm) needles, pick up and k86(88,92,94)sts. evenly around armhole.

· FINISHING ·

Join side and armhole edging seams.

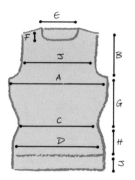

A	17	(17¾,	18¾,	19½)	in
	43	(45,	47.5,	49.5)	cm
B	7¼	(7½,	7¾,	8)	in
	19	(19.5,	20,	20.5)	cm
C	12¼	(13,	14,	15)	in
	31	(33,	36,	38)	cm
D	14	(15,	16,	17)	in
	36	(38,	41,	43)	cm
E	5½	(6,	6,	6¼)	in
	14	(15,	15,	16)	cm
F	3½	(3½,	4,	4)	in
	9	(9,	10,	10)	cm
G	8	(8¼,	8½,	8¾)	in
	20.5	(21,	21.5,	22)	cm
H	1¾				in
	4.5				cm
I	2¾				in
	7				cm
J	14	(14½,	15½,	16)	in
	36	(37,	39,	40)	cm

This close-fitting cable-knit men's sweater has set-in sleeves and a round neck. Made in sport-weight yarn, the eight-row cable and stockinette-stitch pattern soon grows. The natural cream yarn shows off the textured detail of the stitch.

· MEASUREMENTS ·

To fit chest 36(40)in/91(102)cm
Actual measurements 39½(45)in/100 (114)cm
Length to shoulders 22(23)in/56 (58.5)cm
Sleeve seam 18½(19)in/47(48)cm

· MATERIALS ·

9(10) × 50g balls Rowan Designer D.K.
A pair each of size 3 (3¼ mm) and size 5 (4 mm) knitting needles
Cable needle

· GAUGE ·

27 sts. and 32 rows to 4 in (10 cm) over cable pattern using size 5 (4 mm) needles.

· SPECIAL ABBREVIATION ·

C6F., Cable 6 Front worked as follows: slip next 3 sts. onto a cable needle and leave at front of work, k3, then k3 from cable needle.

· BACK ·

Using size 3 (3¼ mm) needles cast on 126(144)sts.
Work 3 in (8 cm) k1, p1 rib.
Change to size 5 (4 mm) needles.
Work in patt. as follows:
Row 1: (Right side) K11(20), * p1, k6,

ROBERT TAYLOR

1911-1969

Robert Taylor, born with the unlikely name of Spangler Arlington Brough in Filley, Nebraska, was the son of a doctor. The cello first attracted him, then the stage, and eventually he was signed by MGM to a seven year contract at the princely sum of $35 a week. He was soon labeled the 'Pretty Boy' of Hollywood, a label he heartily disliked for he was an actor who respected his profession and always tried to give his best. However, his good looks did not hinder his career and undoubtedly helped him get a starring role opposite the great Greta Garbo in *Camille* (1937) and every other major female MGM star for the next two decades.

Taylor was a consistent worker, not wildly ambitious, and stayed with the same studio (MGM) for 25 years. He made many memorably romantic movies such as *Waterloo Bridge* (1940) with Vivien Leigh, *Quo Vadis* (1951) with Deborah Kerr and *Quentin Durward* (1955) with the irrepressible Kay Kendall. His marriage to one of his leading ladies, Barbara Stanwyck, in 1939 lasted 13 years, worth mentioning as its longevity was unusual in Tinsel Town.

His striking and flawless features were complemented by a good physique and he was equally at home in costume, or a contemporary cable-knit pullover, looking classically elegant in both. His stunning good looks and appealing modesty endeared him to millions of female fans throughout his career. Although he would have denied it, he became an institution, firmly entrenched as one of the great glamor stars of Hollywood.

p1, k4, rep. from * to last 7(16)sts., k to end.
Row 2: P7(16), * p4, k1, p6, k1, rep. from * to last 11(20)sts., p to end.
Rows 3 and 4: As rows 1 and 2.
Row 5: K11(20), * p1, C6F, p1, k4, rep. from * to last 7(16)sts., k to end.
Row 6: As row 2.
Rows 7 and 8: As rows 1 and 2.
These 8 rows form the patt.
Continuing in patt., inc. and work into st.st. 1 st. each end of next and every following 16th row until there are 136(154)sts.
Work even until back measures 13½ (14)in/34.5(35.5)cm from beg., ending with a wrong-side row.
Shape armholes
Keeping patt. correct, bind off 4 sts. at beg. of next 2 rows.
Dec. 1 st. each end of next and every following alternate row until 120 (136)sts. remain.
Work even until back measures 22 (23)in/56(58.5)cm from beg., ending with a wrong-side row.
Shape shoulders
Bind off 9(11)sts. at beg. of next 6 rows, then 10(11) sts. at beg. of following 2 rows.
Break off yarn and leave remaining 46(48)sts. on a holder.

· FRONT ·

Work as given for back until front measures 26 rows less than back to beg. of shoulder shaping, ending with a wrong-side row.
Shape neck
Next row: Keeping patt. correct, patt. 52(54)sts., turn and leave remaining sts. on a spare needle.
Work on first set of sts. as follows:
Row 1: Bind off 3 sts., patt. to end.
Row 2: Patt. to end.
Row 3: Bind off 2 sts., patt. to end.
Row 4: Patt. to end.
Rows 5 and 6: As rows 3 and 4.

ROBERT TAYLOR
1911-1969

Dec. 1 st. at beg. of next and every following alternate row until 37 (44)sts. remain, ending at armhole edge.

Patt. 4(14) rows.

Shape shoulder

Bind off 9(11)sts. at beg. of next and following 2 alternate rows.

Work 1 row then bind off.

Return to remaining sts.

With right side facing, slip first 16 (18)sts. onto a holder, join on yarn and patt. to end.

Patt. 1 row.

Now complete 2nd side of neck to match first, reversing all shaping.

· SLEEVES ·

Using size 3 (3¼ mm) needles cast on 54(60)sts.

Work 3 in (8 cm) k1, p1 rib.

Inc. row: Rib 2(6), * M1, rib 1, rep. from * to last 2(6)sts., M1, rib to end: 104(108)sts.

Change to size 5 (4 mm) needles.

Work in patt. as follows:

Row 1: K24(26), * p1, k6, p1, k4, rep. from * to last 32(34)sts., p1, k6, p1, k to end.

Row 2: P24(26), k1, p6, k1, * p4, k1, p6, k1, rep. from * to last 32(34)sts., k1, p6, k1, p to end.

Rows 3 and 4: As rows 1 and 2.

Row 5: K24(26), * p1, C6F, p1, k4, rep. from * to last 32(34)sts., p1, C6F, p1, k to end.

Row 6: As row 2.

Rows 7 and 8: As rows 1 and 2.

These 8 rows form the patt.

Continue in patt. until work measures 18½(19)in/47(48)cm from beg., ending with a wrong-side row.

Shape top

Bind off 4 sts. at beg. of next 2 rows and 2 sts. at beg. of next 4 rows.

Dec. 1 st. at beg. of next 22(26) rows: sts.

Bind off 2 sts. at beg. of next 6 rows, 3 sts. at beg. of next 4 rows, 4 sts. at beg. of next 2 rows, then 5 sts. at beg. of next 2 rows.

Bind off remaining 24 sts.

· NECKBAND ·

Join right shoulder seam.

With right side facing and using size 3 (3¼ mm) needles, pick up and k30(31)sts. down left side of front neck, k across 16(18)sts. from front neck holder, pick up and k30(31)sts. up left side of front neck, then k across 46(48)sts. from back neck holder: 122(128)sts.

Work 1 in (2.5 cm) in k1, p1 rib.

Bind off loosely in rib.

· FINISHING ·

Join left shoulder and neckband seam. Sew in sleeves. Join side and sleeve seams. Press lightly following instructions on ball band.

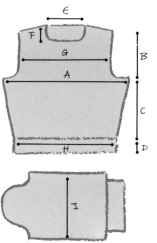

A	20	(22½)	in
	50	(57)	cm
B	8½	(9¼)	in
	21.5	(23)	cm
C	10½	(11)	in
	26.5	(27.5)	cm
D	3¼		in
	8		cm
E	6¾	(7)	in
	17	(18)	cm
F	3¼		in
	8		cm
G	17½	(19½)	in
	44	(50)	cm
H	18½	(21)	in
	47	(53)	cm
I	11	(15¾)	in
	28	(40)	cm
J	15½	(15¾)	in
	39	(40)	cm
K	3¼		in
	8		cm

This short-sleeved summer top made in cool crochet cotton has a deep double-ribbed waist-band. The top is knitted in basic stockinette stitch with a front neck opening and collar. The collar is edged with single crochet to give it shape, and the sleeves have pretty crochet borders.

· MEASUREMENTS ·

To fit bust 32(34,36,38,40)in/81(86, 91,97,102)cm
Actual measurements 33½(36,38,40 42)in/85(91,96,101,107)cm
Length to shoulders 19½(20,20½, 21½,22½)in/50(51,52,55,57)cm
Sleeve seam 5 in (12 cm)

· MATERIALS ·

6(7,8,9,10) × 25g balls Galler Parisienne Cotton
A pair each of size 0 (2 mm) and size 2 (3 mm) knitting needles
Size D (3.00 mm) crochet hook

· GAUGE ·

30 sts. and 38 rows to 4 in (10 cm) over st.st. using size 2 (3 mm) needles.

· BACK ·

* Using size 0 (2 mm) needles cast on 116(120,128,136,144)sts.
Work 4 in (10 cm) k2, p2 rib.
Change to size 2 (3 mm) needles.
Working in st.st., inc. 1 st. each end of 9th and every following 8th row until there are 128(136,144,152,160)sts.
Work even until back measures 13 (13,13,14,14½)in / 33(33,33,36,37)cm, ending with a p row. *
Shape armholes
Bind off 8 sts. at beg. of next 2 rows.

LANA TURNER

1920 ☞

One of Turner's most famous roles as a suburban mother and sexually repressed widow in *Peyton Place* (1958), which earned her an Oscar nomination, is light years away from her usual image of sexy film star and Hollywood glamor queen.

But this 'archetypal' movie princess had a difficult upbringing, often living in near poverty. However, in her midteens she was reputedly discovered in a drug store and propelled towards stardom.

In her early career, the public did not respond to her enthusiastically, but with the help of the legendary Hollywood publicity campaign, she was publicized as 'The Sweater Girl' in *They Won't Forget* (1937), filling an ordinary sweater as never before. All this made her a natural pin-up for U.S. troops entering World War II.

Her popularity gained her a part in *Ziegfeld Girl* (1941) with Judy Garland and Hedy Lamarr. Other films followed thick and fast and the girl from the 'Cinderella' background eventually became one of MGM's top ladies of the 1940s with box office hits like *The Postman Always Rings Twice* (1946) and *The Three Musketeers* (1948).

The public interest in Turner was not always directed towards her movies – her private life was even more colorful. Her seven marriages and numerous love affairs were guaranteed to hold the interest of the public and did for four decades.

This smouldering, tantalizing *femme fatale* exuded sex and glamor whatever she wore. She imbued all clothes with her own personality: spangled gowns, tailored suits, bathrobes and bathing-suits, all spelled Lana Turner.

Dec. 1 st. at each end of next and every following alternate row until 98(104, 110,116,122)sts. remain.
Work even until armholes measure 6½(7,7½,7½,8)in / 17(18,19,19,20)cm from beg. of shaping, ending with a p row.
Shape shoulders
Bind off 6(6,7,7,8)sts. at beg. of next 6 rows, then 5(7,6,8,7)sts. at beg. of following 2 rows.
Break off yarn and leave remaining 52(54,56,58,60)sts. on a holder.

· FRONT ·

Work as given for back from * to *.
Shape armholes and divide for front opening:
Row 1: Bind off 8 sts., k60(64,68, 72,76)sts., turn and leave remaining 60(64,68,72,76)sts. on a spare needle.
Continue on first set of sts. as follows:
Next row: Cast on 8 sts., p across these 8 sts., then p7, k1, p to end.
Next row: K2 tog, k to last 16 sts., p1, k to end.
Continuing to work the 16th st. from neck edge in rev.st.st., dec. 1 st. at armhole edge on every following alternate row until 61(64,67,70,73)sts, remain.
Keeping patt. correct, work even until front measures 18 rows less than back to beg. of shoulder shaping, so ending at armhole edge.
Shape neck
Next 2 rows: K to last 25(26,27, 28,29)sts., turn and p to end.
Next 2 rows: K to last 28(29,30, 31,32)sts., turn and p to end.
Next 2 rows: K to last 31(32,33, 34,35)sts., turn and p to end.
Next 2 rows: K to last 33(34,35, 36,37)sts., turn and p to end.
Next 2 rows: K to last 35(36,37, 38,39)sts., turn and p to end.
Next row: K 23(25,27,29,31)sts., turn and leave remaining sts. on a holder.

Next row: P to end.
Continue in st.st. on these sts. until front measures same as back to beg. of shoulder shaping, ending at armhole edge.

Shape shoulder
Bind off 6(6,7,7,8)sts. at beg. of next and following 2 alternate rows.
Work 1 row, then bind off.
Using size 2 (3 mm) needles cast on 2 sts. for center front border.
K 1 row and p 1 row.
Continuing in st.st., inc. 1 st.at beg. of next 6 rows: 8 sts.
Work 2 rows st.st.
Return to remaining sts.
With right side facing, and using the needle holding the 8 border sts., k across sts. from spare needle for right side of neck: 68(72,76,80,84)sts.

Shape armhole
Next row: Bind off 8 sts., p to last 8 sts., k1, p7, turn and cast on 8 sts. for front border facing: 68(72,76,80, 84)sts.
Continuing to work the 16th st. from neck edge in rev.st.st., dec. 1 st. at armhole edge on next and every following alternate row until 61(64,67, 70,73)sts. remain.
Keeping patt. correct, work even until front measures 18 rows less than back to beg. of shoulder shaping, so ending at armhole edge.

Shape neck
Next 2 rows: P to last 25(26,27, 28,29)sts., turn and k to end.
Next 2 rows: P to last 28(29,30, 31,32)sts., turn and k to end.
Next 2 rows: P to last 31(32,33, 34,35)sts., turn and k to end.
Next 2 rows: P to last 33(34,35, 36,37)sts., turn and k to end.
Next 2 rows: P to last 35(36,37, 38,39)sts., turn and k to end.
Next row: P23(25,27,29,31)sts., turn and leave remaining sts. on a holder.
Next row: K to end.
Continue in st.st. on these sts. until front measures same as back to beg. of

shoulder shaping, ending at armhole edge.
Shape shoulder
Bind off 6(6,7,7,8)sts. at beg. of next and following 2 alternate rows.
Work 1 row, then bind off.

· S L E E V E S ·

Using size 0 (2 mm) needles cast on 84(90,98,102,106)sts.
Beg. k row, work 6 rows st.st.
Change to size 2 (3 mm) needles.
Continue in st.st., inc. 1 st. each end of 3rd and every following 4th row until there are 98(104,112,112,120)sts.
Work even until sleeve measures 4½ in (11 cm) from beg., ending with a p row.
Shape top
Bind off 8 sts. at beg. of next 2 rows.
Dec. 1 st. each end of next and every following alternate row until 68(72, 78,76,82)sts. remain, then dec. 1 st. each end of every row until 30(32, 34,36,38)sts. remain.
Bind off 4 sts. at beg. of next 4 rows.
Bind off.

· C O L L A R ·

Join shoulder seams.
Slip the first 8 sts. at neck edges onto safety-pins for borders.
With wrong side facing and using size 0 (2 mm) needles, k across 30(31,32,33, 34)sts. from left front neck holder, pick up and k10(11,12,13,14)sts. up left side of neck, k across 52(54,56, 58,60)sts. from back neck holder, pick up and k10(11,12,13,14)sts. down right side of neck, then k across 30(31,32, 33,34)sts. from right front neck holder: 132(138,144,150,156)sts.
Beg. p row, work 9 rows st.st.
Change to size 2 (3 mm) needles.
Shape back collar
Row 1: K to last 8 sts., turn.
Row 2: P to last 8 sts., turn.

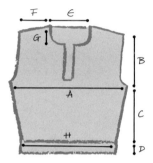

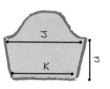

A	16½	(17¾,	19,	19¾,	21)	in
	42.5	(45.5,	48,	50.5,	53.5)	cm
B	6¾	(7,	7½,	7½,	7¾)	in
	17	(18,	19,	19,	20)	cm
C	9	(9,	9,	10¼,	10¾)	in
	23	(23,	23,	26,	27)	cm
D	4	in
	10	cm
E	6¾	(7,	7¼,	7½,	7¾)	in
	17	(18,	19,	19.5,	20)	cm
F	3	(3¼,	3½,	3¾,	4)	in
	8	(8.5,	9,	9.5,	10)	cm
G	2½	in
	6.5	cm
H	15½	(15¾,	17,	17¾,	19)	in
	39	(40,	43,	45,	48)	cm
I	12¾	(13½,	14¾,	14¾,	15¾)	in
	32.5	(34.5,	37.5,	37.5,	40)	cm
J	4¼	in
	11	cm
K	11	(12,	12¾,	13½,	14)	in
	28	(30,	32.5,	34,	35.5)	cm

Continue in this way, working 8 sts. less on every row until the row – p to last 32 sts., turn – has been worked.

Next row: K to end.

Next row: P to end.

Continue in st.st. until collar measures 4 in (10 cm) from beg., measured up front edge.

Inc. 1 st. each end of next and every following 4th row until there are 142(148,154,160,166)sts.

Work 3 more rows st.st.

Bind off.

· FINISHING ·

Slip 8 sts. from safety-pins onto a size 2 (3 mm) needle, join on yarn and bind off.

Fold facings to wrong side and slip stitch in place. Sew down lower edge of left border behind right, then stitch shaped edge of right border neatly into place at front. Sew in sleeves. Join side and sleeve seams.

With right side of collar facing and using a size D (3.00 mm) crochet hook, work 1 row sc. round collar edge. Fasten off.

Fold ¼ in (5 mm) to wrong side right round collar edges and slipstitch into place.

Sleeve edging: With right side facing, work 1 round of sc. evenly round sleeve edge, working a multiple of 6 sts., join with a ss.

Next row: * Miss 2 sc., 5 dc. into next sc., miss 2 sc., ss. into next sc., rep. from * to end. Fasten off.

This simple sleeveless top has a cigarette motif – once the epitome of chic – knitted from a chart with the glowing ends embroidered in orange satin stitch. You can substitute your own motif if you prefer or knit it plain. The round neck and armholes are edged with narrow single-rib borders.

· MEASUREMENTS ·

To fit bust 30(32,34,36,38,40)in/76 (81,86,91,97,102)cm
Actual measurements 27(29,31,33, 35½,37½)in/69(74,79,84,90,95)cm
Length 21¼(21¼,21½,22,22¼)in/54 (54.5,55,56,56.5)cm

· MATERIALS ·

3(4,4,5,5,6) × 50g balls Emu Superwash 4 ply in main color A
Oddments of white (contrast color B) for cigarette motif
Oddments of orange (contrast color C) for embroidering cigarette ends
A pair each of size 1 (2¾ mm) and size 3 (3¼ mm) knitting needles

· GAUGE ·

28 sts. and 36 rows to 4 in (10 cm) over st.st. using size 3 (3¼ mm) needles.

· BACK ·

* Using size 1 (2¾ mm) needles and A, cast on 83(89,97,103,111,117)sts.
Rib row 1: K1, * p1, k1, rep. from * to end.
Rib row 2: P1, * k1, p1, rep. from * to end.
Rep these 2 rows for 2 in (5 cm), ending with rib row 2.
Change to size 3 (3¼ mm) needles.
Proceed in st.st. increasing 1 st. each

JANE WYMAN

1914 ☞

The ex-Mrs Ronald Reagan, was born Sara Jane Faulks in St Joseph, Missouri. Today, as Jane Wyman, she is best known for her powerful performance as the tragic deaf-mute in *Johnny Belinda* (1948). This film was the turning point of her career since up until then she played mostly in B films or was the heroine's best friend, playing with such big stars as Olivia de Havilland. When she eventually attained stardom (and an Oscar) for *Johnny Belinda* a new Wyman emerged; in forever playing brassy blonde roles her genuine talents had been submerged. She went on to work with Hitchcock in *Stage Fright* (1950) but they didn't hit it off – he wanted her to look plain for the part of a drama student in London but she had other ideas.

Hollywood decided she had taste, intelligence and professionalism in the first degree. If any actress deserved an award for sheer tenacity and the will to succeed, it must surely be Jane Wyman! She went on to make movie after movie, three of the most popular being *Magnificent Obsession* (1954), and *All that Heaven Allows* (1955) with Rock Hudson, and *Miracle in the Rain* (1956) opposite Van Johnson. Her film popularity declined at the end of the 1950s, but she now appears in the popular television 'soap' *Falcon Crest*.

Jane Wyman has curious good looks, somewhat oriental at certain angles. Her look is very 1950s with sharply outlined red lips, slightly snub nose and well-defined angles to the face. She is always stylish and soignée, tempered with an attractive natural warmth.

end of 3rd and every following 6th row until there are 97(103,111,117,127, 133)sts.
Work even until back measures 13 in (33 cm) from cast-on edge, ending with a p row.
Place a marker at each end of last row to denote beg. of armholes. *
Work even until armholes measure 8¼(8½,8½,9,9,9¼)in/21(21.5,22,22.5, 23,23.5)cm from markers, ending with a p row.
Shape shoulders
Bind off 12(13,15,16,18,19)sts. at beg. of next 4 rows.
Cut off yarn and leave remaining 49(51,51,53,55,57)sts. on a holder.

· FRONT ·

Work as given for back from * to *.
Work 14 rows st.st.
Use separate small balls of yarn for each area of color and twist yarns together on wrong side of work when changing color to avoid making a hole. Reading odd numbered (k) rows from right to left and even numbered (p) rows from left to right, proceed to position patt. from chart as follows:
Row 1: (Right side) K18(21,25,28, 33,36)A, working from chart k18A, 1B, 2A, then with A k58(61,65,68, 73,76).
Row 2: P58(61,65,68,73,76)A, working from chart p1A, 4B, 16A, then with A, p18(21,25,28,33,36)A.
Continue in patt. from chart until row 31 has been completed.
Continuing in A only, work even until armholes measure 6(6¼,6½,6½, 6½,7)in/15.5(16,16.5,16.5,17,17.5)cm from markers, ending with a p row.
Shape neck
Next row: K34(37,41,43,47,50), turn and leave remaining sts. on a spare needle.
Work on first set of sts. as follows:
Dec. 1 st. at neck edge on every row

JANE WYMAN

1914 ☞

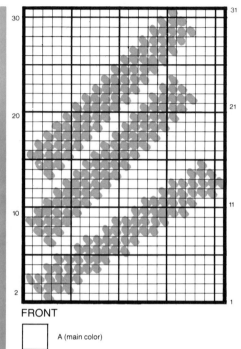

FRONT

	A (main color)
	B (contrast color, white)

until 24(26,30,32,36,38)sts. remain.
Work even until front measures the
same length as back to shoulders, ending at armhole edge.

Shape shoulder
Bind off 12(13,15,16,18,19)sts. at beg.
of next row.
Work one row. Bind off.
Return to sts. on spare needle.
With right side facing, slip first
29(29,29,31,33,33)sts. onto a holder,
join A to next st. and k to end of row;
34(37,41,43,47,50)sts.
Now complete to match first side of
neck.

· NECKBAND ·

Join right shoulder seam.
With right side facing, join A to neck
at left front shoulder and using size 1
(2¾ mm) needles, pick up and k25
(25,26,26,27,27)sts. down left side
of front neck, k the front neck sts. from
holder, pick up and k25(25,26,26,27,
27)sts. up right side of front neck, then

k the back neck sts. from holder:
128(130,132,136,142,144)sts.
Work 5 rows k1, p1 rib.
Bind off in rib.

· ARMHOLE BORDERS ·

Join left shoulder and neckband seam.
With right side facing, join A to
armhole at one marker and using size
1 (2¾ mm) needles, pick up and
k116(120,122,126,128,132)sts. evenly
between markers.
Work 5 rows k1, p1 rib.
Bind off in rib.

· FINISHING ·

See ball band for pressing and
washing details.
Join side and armhole border seams.
Using satin stitch and C, embroider
tips of cigarettes.

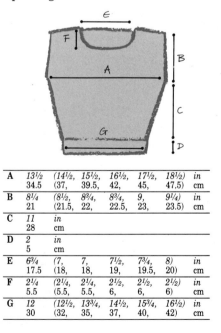

A	13½ 34.5	(14½, (37,	15½, 39.5,	16½, 42,	17½, 45,	18½) 47.5)	in cm
B	8¼ 21	(8½, (21.5,	8¾, 22,	8¾, 22.5,	9, 23,	9¼) 23.5)	in cm
C	11 28						in cm
D	2 5						in cm
E	6¾ 17.5	(7, (18,	7, 18,	7½, 19,	7¾, 19.5,	8) 20)	in cm
F	2¼ 5.5	(2¼, (5.5,	2¼, 5.5,	2½, 6,	2½, 6,	2½) 6)	in cm
G	12 30	(12½, (32,	13¾, 35,	14½, 37,	15¾, 40,	16½) 42)	in cm

This jacket-style cardigan with set-in sleeves is worked in a chunky cable pattern. Instructions are given for knitting or crocheting the neck and button borders. Two tabs with button trims on the left shoulder complete the tailored look of this cardigan.

· MEASUREMENTS ·

To fit bust 32(34,36,38)in/81(86,91, 97)cm

Actual measurements 36½(38½,41 43½)in/93(98,104,110)cm

Length to shoulders 21¼(21½,22, 22½)in/54(55,56,57)cm

Sleeve seam 16½(17,17¼,17½)in/42 43,44,45)cm

· MATERIALS ·

15(15,16,16) × 50g Phildar Satine 4

A pair each of size 2 (3 mm) and size 5 (4 mm) knitting needles

Size E (3.50 mm) crochet hook (for optional crocheted borders)

Cable needle

10 buttons

· GAUGE ·

26 sts. and 29 rows to 4 in (10 cm) over cable pattern using size 5 (4 mm) needles.

· SPECIAL ABBREVIATION FOR CROCHETED BORDERS ·

Rtr., Raised treble worked as follows: insert hook round stem of next stitch, working from the front on right-side rows and working from the back on wrong-side rows, then work a treble in the normal way, so that the treble is 'raised up' on the right side of the work.

LORETTA YOUNG

1 9 1 3 ☞

Loretta Young was born in the Mormon Capital, Salt Lake City but moved to Hollywood with her mother and three sisters when she was four. She acted in her first films while still a child, but her film career began in earnest when as a teenager she was hired out as an extra to various film studios. This work culminated in a contract with Warner Brothers in 1929 where they teamed her successfully in several movies with the famous star Douglas Fairbanks Jr.

Loretta was always a glamorous and pretty woman with a face the camera loved. She was also a designer's dream, and certainly knew about clothes on and off screen. She was at her best when her roles required her to dress with style and indeed she had many opportunities to wear flattering, extravagant costumes; in *House of Rothschild* (1934) she looked perfect in high-waisted Regency dresses while in *Suez* (1938) she looked equally at home playing the empress Eugenie in full crinoline.

In her early film career she often played down-trodden, poverty-stricken heroines – but they were always beautiful and they always had class.

Her versatility and good looks, together with her accessible stylishness, ensured her a long and successful career. Her award-winning TV series *The Loretta Young Show* (1953 –61) was particularly remarkable for the chic outfits that she wore.

Still around to tell the tale today with a recent television appearance to her credit, she is undoubtedly one of the aristocrats of Hollywood.

· BACK ·

Using size 2 (3 mm) needles cast on 91(95,101,107)sts.

Rib row 1: P1, * k1, p1, rep. from * to end.

Rib row 2: K1, * p1, k1, rep. from * to end.

Rep these 2 rows for 4 in (10 cm), ending with rib row 1.

Inc. row: Rib 3(1,2,2,), * inc. in next st., rib 2, rep. from * to last 4(4,3,3), inc. in next 1(3,1,1)sts., rib 3(1,2,2): 120(128,134,142)sts.

Change to size 5 (4 mm) needles.

Work in patt. as follows:

Row 1: K to end.

Row 2: P to end.

Rows 3 and 4: As rows 1 and 2.

Row 5: K2, [C4F] 2(3,2,3) times, * k2, [C4F] 3 times, rep. from * to last 12(2,12,2)sts., k2(0,2,0), [C4F] 2(0,2,0) times, k2.

Row 6: P to end.

These 6 rows form the patt.

Continue in patt. until back measures 14 in (35 cm) from beg, ending with a wrong-side row.

Shape armholes

Bind off 3(4,4,4)sts. at beg. of next 2(2,2,4) rows.

Bind off 2(3,3,3)sts. at beg. of next 2(2,4,2) rows, then bind off 2 sts. at beg. of next 2(4,2,2) rows.

Dec. 1 st. at beg. of next and every following row until 100(102,106, 108)sts. remain.

Work even until back measures 21¼ (21½,22,22½)in/54(55,56,57)cm from beg., ending with a wrong-side row.

Shape shoulders and neck

Bind off 7 sts. at beg. of next 2 rows, then 7(7,7,8)sts. at beg. of following 2 rows.

Next row: Bind off 7(7,8,8)sts., patt. until there are 16(17,18,18)sts. on needle, bind off next 26 sts., patt. to end.

Work on first side of neck as follows:

Next row: Bind off 7(7,8,8)sts., patt.

LORETTA YOUNG
1913 ☞

to end.

Next row: Bind off 9(9,10,10)sts., patt. to end.

Bind off remaining 7(8,8,8)sts.

Return to remaining sts.

With wrong side facing, rejoin yarn and complete second side of neck to match first, reversing all shaping.

· RIGHT FRONT ·

Using size 2 (3 mm) needles cast on 44(46,50,52)sts.

Rib row 1: K2, * p1, k1, rep. from * to end.

Rib row 2: P1, * k1, p1, rep. from * to last st., k1.

Rep. these 2 rows for 4 in (10 cm), ending with rib row 1.

Inc. row: Rib 1(7,1,8), * inc. in next st., rib 2(1,2,1), rep. from * to last 1(7,1,8)sts., inc. in next st., rib 0(6,0,7): 59(63,67,71)sts.

Change to size 5 (4 mm) needles.

Work in patt. as follows:

Row 1: K to end.

Row 2: P to end.

Rows 3 and 4: As rows 1 and 2.

Row 5: K1, [C4F] 1(1,3,3) times, * k2, [C4F] 3 times, rep. from * to last 12(2, 12,2)sts., k2(0,2,0), [C4F] 2(0,2,0) times, k2.

Row 6: P to end.

These 6 rows form the patt.

Continue in patt. until work measures 14 in (35 cm) from beg., ending at side edge.

Shape armhole

Shape armhole as given for back, then work even until front measures 19 (19¼,19½,20)in/48(49,50,51)cm from beg., ending at center front edge: 49 (50,53,54)sts.

Shape neck

Next row: Bind off 5 sts., patt. to end.

Bind off 3(3,4,4)sts. at neck edge on following alternate row, then 3 sts. at beg. of following alternate row and 2 sts. at beg. of following 3(3,4,4) alter-

nate rows.

Dec. 1 st. at neck edge at beg. of following 4(4,3,3) alternate rows.

Shape shoulder

Bind off 7 sts. at beg. of next row, 7(7,7,8)sts. at beg. of following alternate row and 7(7,8,8)sts. at beg. of following alternate row. Work 1 row, then bind off.

· LEFT FRONT ·

Work as given for right front, reversing patt. on row 5 as follows:

Row 5: K2, [C4F] 2(3,2,3) times, * k2, [C4F] 3 times, rep. from * to last 7(7,1,1)sts., k2(2,0,0), [C4F] 1(1,0,0) time, k1.

Now continuing in patt. as set, complete to match right front, reversing all shaping.

· SLEEVES ·

Using size 2 (3 mm) needles cast on 50(54,58,62)sts.

Work 2½ in (6 cm) k1, p1 rib, ending with a right-side row.

Inc. row: Rib 8(1,3,5), * inc. in next st., rib 1(2,2,2), rep. from * to last 8(2,4,6)sts., inc. in next st., rib to end: 68(72,76,80)sts.

Change to size 5 (4 mm) needles.

Work in patt. as follows:

Row 1: K to end.

Row 2: P to end.

Rows 3 and 4: As rows 1 and 2.

Row 5: Inc. in first st., k0(2,0,2), [C4F] 1(1,2,2) times, * k2, [C4F] 3 times, rep. from * to last 7(9,11,13)sts., k2, [C4F] 1(1,2,2) times, k0(2,0,2), inc. in last st.

Row 6: P to end.

Continue in patt. as set, increasing and working into patt. 1 st. each end of 6th and every following 4th row until there are 116(120,124,128)sts.

Work even until sleeve measures 16½ (17,17½,18)in/42(43,44,45)cm from beg., ending with a wrong-side row.

Shape top

Bind off 3(4,4,4)sts. at beg. of next 2 rows, then 2 sts. at beg. of next 12(12,14,16) rows: 86(88,88,88)sts.

Dec. 1 st at beg. of next 18(20,20,20) rows: 68 sts.

Bind off 2 sts. at beg. of next 10 rows, 3 sts. at beg. of following 4 rows, then 4 sts. at beg. of following 4 rows.

Bind off remaining 20 sts.

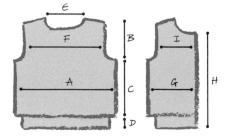

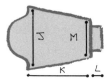

A	18	(19¼,	20,	21¼)	in
	46	(49,	51,	54)	cm
B	7½	(7¾,	8¼,	8¾)	in
	19	(20,	21,	22)	cm
C	9¾				in
	25				cm
D	4				in
	10				cm
E	6¾	(6¾,	7,	7)	in
	17	(17,	18,	18)	cm
F	15	(15¼,	15¾,	16)	in
	38	(39,	40,	41)	cm
G	9¼	(9¾,	10¼,	10¾)	in
	23	(25,	26,	27)	cm
H	19	(19¼,	19½,	20)	in
	48	(49,	50,	51)	cm
I	7¾	(7¾,	8,	8)	in
	20	(20,	20.5,	20.5)	cm
J	17¾	(18,	19,	19¼)	in
	45	(46,	48,	49)	cm
K	14	(14½,	15,	15½)	in
	36	(37,	38,	39)	cm
L	2¼				in
	6				cm
M	10¼	(11,	11½,	12¼)	in
	26	(28,	29,	31)	cm

· CROCHETED NECKBAND ·

Join shoulder seams.
With right side facing and using size E (3.50 mm) crochet hook, work 85(85, 89,89) hdc. evenly round neck edge.
Next row: 2 ch. (to count as first dc.), * 1 dc. round next st., 1 dc. into next st., rep. from * to last 2 sts., 1 dc. into each of last 2 sts.
Next row: 2 ch. (to count as first dc.), * 1 dc. into Rdc., 1 Rdc. round next dc., rep. from * to last 2 sts., 1 dc. into each of last 2 sts.
Rep. these 2 rows twice more.
Fasten off.

· CROCHETED BUTTONHOLE BORDER ·

With right side facing and using size E (3.50 mm) hook, work 103(105,107, 109) hdc. evenly along right front edge.
Next row: 2 ch. (to count as first dc.), * 1 Rdc. round next st., 1 dc. into next st., rep. from * to end.
Continuing in patt. as for neckband, work 2 more rows, then work buttonholes on next row as follows:
Next row: (Right side) 2 ch. (to count as first dc.), patt. across 5(7,8,4) sts., * 2 ch., miss 2 sts., patt. across 11(11, 11,12) sts., rep. from * 6 times more, 2 ch., miss 2 sts., patt. to end.
Next row: Patt. to end, working 2 hdc. into 2 ch. sps.
Next row: Patt. to end.
Fasten off.

· CROCHETED BUTTON BORDER ·

Work as given for buttonhole border, omitting buttonholes.

· CROCHETED TABS ·

Using size E (3.50 mm) hook make 15 ch.
1 sc. into 2nd ch. from hook, 1 sc. into each sc. to end.
Work 4 rows sc., then fasten off.

· KNITTED NECKBAND ·

Join shoulder seams.
With right side facing and using size 2 (3 mm) needles, pick up and k91(91,95, 95) sts. evenly round neck edge.
Work in Irish moss st. as follows:
Row 1: P1, * k1, p1, rep. from * to end.
Row 2: * K1, p1, rep. from * to last st., k1.
Row 3: As row 2.
Row 4: As row 1.
Rep these 4 rows until neckband measures 1½ in (4 cm), ending with a wrong-side row.
Bind off in patt.

· KNITTED BUTTONHOLE BORDER ·

With right side facing and using size 2 (3 mm) needles, pick up and k115(117, 121,123) sts. evenly along right front edge.
Work rows 1 to 4 of Irish moss st. as given for neckband, then work rows 1 and 2 again.
Buttonhole row: (Wrong side) Patt. 3(4,3,4), * bind off 2 sts., patt. until there are 13(13,14,14) sts. on needle after bind-off sts., rep. from * 6 times more, bind off 2 sts., patt. to end.
Next row: Patt. to end, casting on 2 sts. over those bound off in previous row.
Work 5 more rows in patt.
Bind off in patt.

· KNITTED BUTTON BORDER ·

Work as given for buttonhole border, omitting buttonholes.

· KNITTED TABS ·

Using size 2 (3 mm) needles cast on 15 sts.
Work 6 rows Irish moss st.
Bind off.

· FINISHING ·

Sew in sleeves, gathering at top to fit. Join side and sleeve seams. Sew on buttons.
Stitch top ends of tabs to left front at just below shoulder level, laying them diagonally towards the armhole.
Sew button to each of lower edges of tabs, stitching through both thicknesses to secure to front.

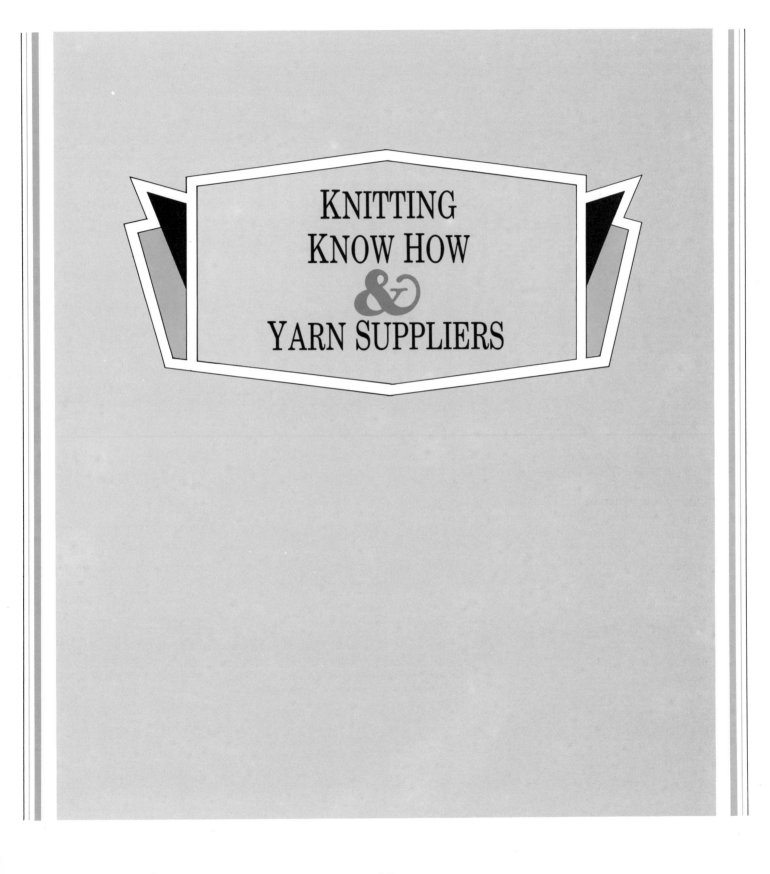

KNITTING
KNOW HOW
&
YARN SUPPLIERS

· ABBREVIATIONS ·

k	knit
p	purl
st(s)	stitch(es)
st st	stockinette stitch
rev st st	reversed stockinette stitch
patt	pattern
rep	repeat
beg	beginning
inc	increase(ing)
dec	decrease(ing)
tog	together
sl	slip
in	inch(es)
mm	millimeters
cm	centimeters
psso	pass slip stitch over
skpo	slip 1, knit 1, pass slip stitch over
tbl	through back of loops
puk	pick up and knit **or** make
or M1	one by picking up the loop between stitch just worked and next stitch on left-hand needle and knitting into the back of it
K1B	knit 1 below by inserting needle into stitch below next stitch on left-hand needle, then knitting it in the usual way, letting the stitch above drop off the needle
C4F	cable 4 front by slipping the next 2 stitches onto a cable needle, knit the next 2 stitches, then knit the 2 stitches from the cable needle
ytf	yarn to front
ytb	yarn to back
sl 1 pw	slip 1 purlwise
tr	treble
Rdc	raised double crochet
ch	chain
dc	double crochet
sc	single crochet
hdc	half double crochet
ss	slip stitch

· GAUGE ·

● The required gauge for a 4in (10cm) square is given at the beginning of each pattern. Unless you knit with the correct gauge there is little chance that your garment will come out the right size.

● To check the gauge, use the stitch, yarn and needles specified in the pattern and knit a sample slightly bigger than 4in (10cm) square. Put the square on a flat surface, taking care not to stretch it and, with pins, mark the number of stitches and then rows (for example 22 sts and 30 rows) required by the pattern to achieve the right gauge. Measure the distance between the pins and, if it is not 4in (10cm), *adjust the gauge.*

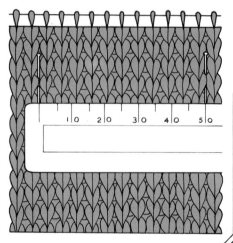

Diagram shows 11 stitches to 5cm

● If, in this example, you have fewer than 22 sts to 10cm, your gauge is too loose. Switch to smaller needles and work another square. If your gauge is too tight, work another square using larger needles.

● The time taken getting your gauge square right is nothing compared to unpicking an entire garment, so keep on experimenting with different needle sizes until your measurements are perfect.

· EMBROIDERY ·

Some of the designs have added embroidery to give extra detail. These are called backstitch, French knots, satin stitch and Lazy Daisy stitch. Backstitch is used when just a straight line is needed, French knots are used for spots or centers of flowers and satin and Lazy Daisy stitches are used to form the petals and leaves of flowers.

Backstitch

● Thread the needle with required colored yarn and fasten at back of work.

● Bring the needle through to the right side of the fabric.

● Insert the needle back through the fabric about ¼ in (5 mm) to the right of where the yarn was brought through and then bring back out again about ¼ in (5 mm) to the left of the first stitch. Draw the needle through, pulling yarn gently.

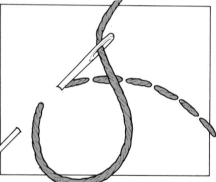

● Now insert the needle back into the fabric at the end of the first stitch and bring out again ¼ in (5 mm) further along.

● Continue in this way until the line has been completed, then fasten off securely.

French Knots

● Thread needle with required colored yarn and fasten at back of work.

● Bring the needle through to the right side of the fabric at the position for the knot. Take a small stitch of the fabric and wind the yarn 2, 3 or 4 times round the point of the needle (depending on how large the knot is to be).

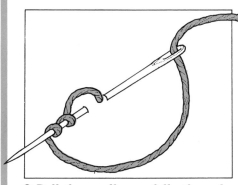

● Pull the needle carefully through, then insert the needle back through the fabric at the base of the knot and fasten off on the wrong side.

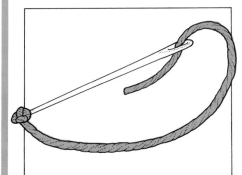

Satin Stitch

● Thread needle with required colored yarn and fasten at back of work.

● Bring the needle through to the right side of the fabric at the position for the start of the area to be covered.

● Lay the yarn over the area to be covered and insert the needle back through the fabric to the wrong side of work.

● Bring the needle back through the fabric, close to the first position that the needle was brought to on the right side.

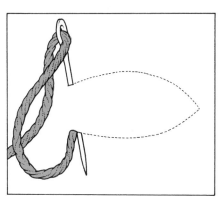

● Insert the needle again over the area to be filled, making sure that the stitches are kept close to each other.

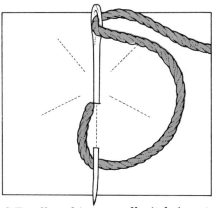

● Continue in this way until the area is filled, taking care to keep the stitches at an even tension so that the surface is smooth and even.

Lazy Daisy Stitch

● Thread needle with required colored yarn and fasten at back of work.

● Bring the needle through to the right side of the fabric at the position for the start of the stitch.

● Take a stitch, the length that you wish the petal or leaf to be, bringing the needle back through to the right side of the fabric.

● Wind the yarn round under the needle point, then draw the needle through.

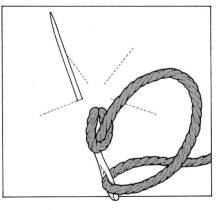

● Finally, taking a small stitch, insert the needle back through the fabric to catch the loop into place.

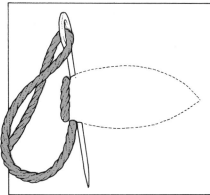

● Work several Lazy Daisy stitches in a circle to form a flower, taking care to keep all the loops the same size, making an even flower head.

● JUDY GAR

● JANE WYMAN ●

Several of the garments in this book are finished with crochet edges, as there are very often no knitted equivalents. A few of the basic stitches are given here.

Chain

● Make a slip loop and place on crochet hook. Place the crochet hook in your right hand, then hold the yarn in your left hand, keeping about 4 in (5 cm) above the knot pulled fairly taut.

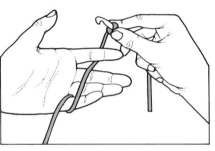

● Hold the slip knot in your left hand and pull gently on this to form the tension. Push the hook under the yarn and back over the top so that a loop of yarn passes over the hook.

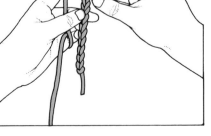

● Draw this loop through the loop already on the hook to form one chain.
● Repeat step 2 over and over to form the chain, pulling it down gently with the left hand to keep the tension even.

Single Crochet

● Make a chain the required length. Insert a hook into the 2nd chain from hook, wind the yarn round the hook and draw a loop through.

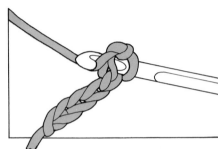

● Wind yarn round hook again and draw through both loops on hook.

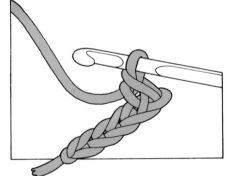

● * Insert hook into next chain, yarn round hook, draw loop through, yarn round hook again, then draw through both loops on hook. Repeat from * to end of row.

● JEAN HARLOW ●

● CLAUDETTE COLBERT ●

● GRETA GARBO ●

Half Double Crochet ·
● Make a chain the required length. Yarn round hook, then insert hook in 3rd chain from hook and draw a loop through.

Double Crochet
● Make a chain the required length. Yarn round hook, then insert hook in 4th chain from hook and draw a loop through.

Slipstitch
This stitch is usually used to join or neaten off the end of a row, or to work along a row, without forming any increase in the height of the fabric, to a given place.

● Yarn round hook again and draw through all three loops on hook.

● Yarn round hook and draw through 2 of the loops on the hook, yarn round hook again and draw through last 2 loops on hook.

● * Insert hook into next stitch, yarn round hook, draw loop through fabric and stitch on hook. Repeat from * to given point.

● * Yarn round hook and insert hook into next chain, yarn round hook again, then draw through all three loops on hook. Repeat from * to end of row.

● * Yarn round hook and insert hook into next chain, yarn round hook and draw through 2 loops, yarn round hook again and draw through last 2 loops. Repeat from * to end of row.

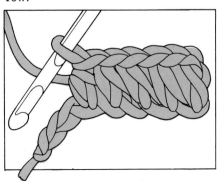

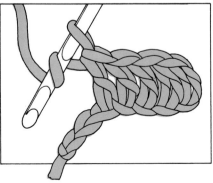

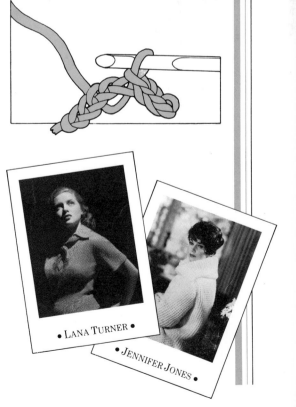

· LANA TURNER ·

· JENNIFER JONES ·

· READING CHARTS ·

● Some of the patterns in this book use charts.

● Each chart consists of a grid, sometimes the actual shape of the piece being knitted, marked up into squares.

● Each square represents one stitch and each horizontal line of squares represents one row.

● Unless otherwise given out in the instructions the design as shown on the chart is worked in stockinette stitch, all odd numbered rows being read from right to left and worked as knit stitches (right-side rows) and all even numbered rows being read from left to right and worked as purl stitches (wrong-side rows).

● Each square shows which color yarn is to be used for that stitch.

● If on the design you are working there is only a small motif to be worked, then the chart is only given for that area of the sweater and the instructions will tell you where to place the motif within the row. All stitches either side of the chart are then worked in the main color.

● If the chart is for the full section of the piece you are knitting, then it will usually indicate any shaping that needs to be done. If the number of squares varies at the side, armhole and neck edges, then increase or decrease that number of stitches at that point on the row you are working.

● At the center front neck, where there are usually quite a few stitches to be shaped, either leave the centre stitches on a holder or refer to the pattern instructions to see if it tells you to bind them off.

· CHANGING COLORS ·

● When working from the charts it is necessary to use several different colors, very often within the same row.

● If there are very small areas to be worked in any of these colors, then wind off a small amount either into a small ball or onto a bobbin. This will make working with a lot of colors easier and help to stop them getting muddled.

● When joining in a new color at the beginning of a row, insert the needle into the first stitch, make a loop in the new yarn, leaving an end to be later woven in, then place this loop over the needle and complete the stitch.

● When joining in a new color in the middle of a row, work in the first color to the point where the new color is needed, then insert the needle into the next stitch and complete with the new color in the same way as for joining in at the beginning of a row.

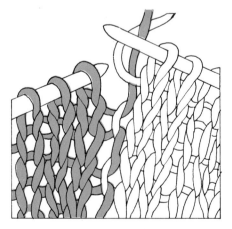

● When changing color along a row always make sure that the color that is being used is twisted around the next color to be used, otherwise the two stitches will not be linked together and a hole will form between them.

· BLOCKING ·

After knitting all the pieces for the garment, first weave in all the ends securely; then for a better finished look block out all the pieces.

● Cover a large area with a thick blanket and a piece of clean fabric such as sheeting.

● Lay out each piece of the garment and pin out to shape.

● If the yarn can be pressed then cover with a damp cloth and press each piece lightly avoiding all ribbing. Do not move the iron over the fabric, but keep picking up and placing it lightly down again.

● If the yarn cannot be pressed then cover with a damp cloth and leave until completely dry.

· CARY GRANT ·

· VIRGINIA MAYO ·

· GARY COOPER ·

Once the pieces have been blocked refer to the finishing instructions for the order in which to assemble them.

When joining seams where the pattern needs to match at any point then the invisible seam method gives a more professional finish, but a backstitched seam is slightly easier and with care can give just as neat a finish.

Invisible seam

● Lay both pieces of fabric to be joined on a flat surface with the right sides facing. Thread the needle with matching yarn and join it to the lower edge of one of the pieces.

● Take the needle and insert it into the center of the first stitch at the lower edge of the second piece of knitting. Bring the needle back up through the stitch above, so picking up the bar between the rows of stitches.

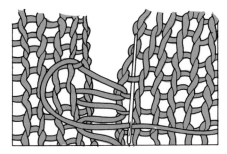

● Pull the yarn through, then take the needle back across to the first piece of knitting and repeat. Pull the yarn gently so that the two pieces of knitting are drawn together. Insert the needle back into the second piece of knitting, in the same place as the needle came out, and pick up the next bar above, then repeat again on the first piece of knitting.

● Continue in this way to the top of the seam, gently pulling the yarn every few stitches to close the seam.

● After the last stitch fasten off securely.

Backstitch seam

● Place the two pieces to be joined right sides together.

● Thread the needle with matching yarn and fasten to beginning of the seam with a couple of stitches.

● Insert the needle through both thicknesses and bring back out again about ¼ in (5 mm) along the seam. Draw the needle through, pulling yarn gently.

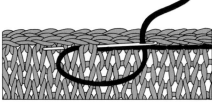

● Insert the needle back into the same place as it was inserted the first time but this time bring out about ¼ in (5 mm) further along from the last stitch. Pull the yarn through.

● Now insert the needle back into the fabric at the end of the first stitch and bring out again ¼ in (5 mm) further along.

Continue in this way to the end of the seam, then fasten off securely.

● After all the hard work of knitting and finishing your garment it is important to wash it correctly in order to keep it looking as new.

● Always keep a ball band from one of the balls of yarn with which the garment was knitted, so that you can refer to the washing instructions for that yarn. If there are no washing instructions on the ball band, or if you have not kept one, then hand wash only in cool water. Either squeeze gently or give a short spin, then lay the garment flat and ease into shape.

● Dry flat away from heat or direct sunlight.

· ROBERT TAYL

· ERROL FLYNN ·

· PEGGY CUMMINS ·

· JOAN CRAWFORD ·

· DOROTHY LAMOUR ·

· ADELE JERGENS ·

· YARN SUPPLIERS ·

All the yarns in this book should be readily obtainable from good yarn suppliers. If you experience difficulty in finding a particular yarn please contact the relevant supplier direct at the address given below.

· CHANDOS ·

USA
Silk City Fibers
155 Oxford Street
Patterson
NJ 07522

CANADA
Silk City Fibers
155 Oxford Street
Patterson
NJ 07522

· EMU ·

USA
Plymouth Yarn Company Inc
PO Box 28
500 Lafayette Street
Bristol
PA 19007

CANADA
S R Kertzer Ltd,
257 Adelaide Street West,
Toronto
Ontario
M5H 1Y1

· GALLER ·

USA
Joseph Galler Inc
27 West 20th Street
New York
NY 10011

CANADA
For Galler Lino Fino please substitute Twilleys Bubbly and for Galler Parisienne Cotton please substitute Twilleys Lyscordet.

S R Kertzer (Twilleys Supplier)
257 Adelaide Street West
Toronto
Ontario
M5H 1Y1

· LISTER·LEE ·

USA
Not available. Please substitute any other knitting worsted yarn.

CANADA
Not available. Please substitute any other knitting worsted yarn.

· GEORGE PICAUD ·

USA
Merino Wool Co Inc
16 West 19th Street
NY 10001

CANADA
Bruneau
338 St Antoine East
Montreal
Quebec H27 1A3

· PINGOUIN ·

USA
Pingouin Corporation
PO Box 100
Highway 45
Jamestown
South Carolina 29453

CANADA
Promofil Canada Limitée
300 Boulevard Laurentien
Suite 100
Saint-Laurent QE
H4M 2L4

· ROBIN ·

USA
Available through Emu supplier.

CANADA
Available through Emu supplier.

· ROWAN ·

USA
Westminster Trading
5 Northern Boulevard
Amherst
New Hampshire 03031

CANADA
Estelle
38 Continental Place
Scarborough
Ontario M1R 2T4

· SCHEEPJESWOL ·

USA
Scheepjeswol USA
199 Trade Zone Drive
Ronkonama NY 11779

CANADA
Scheepjeswol (Canada) Ltd
400 B Montée de Liesse
Montreal
Quebec H4T 1N8

· PHILDAR ·

USA
Phildar Inc
6438 Dawson Boulevard
85 North
Norcross
Georgia 30093

CANADA
Phildar Limitée
6200 Est
Boulevard H Bourassa
Montreal Nord
HIG 5X3

· ACKNOWLEDGEMENTS ·

*The author and publishers acknow-
ledge with thanks the cooperation of
the following:*

**Metro Goldwyn Mayer, Twentieth
Century Fox, Warner Brothers,
RKO, Paramount, Goldwyn,
Columbia, United Artists**

**Thanks to Christine and Cheryl
for their research.**

· MARILYN MONROE ·

· JANE GREER ·

· LORETTA YOUNG ·